Deciphering the Bitcoin Blueprint

Mastering Bitcoin: Strategies for Success in the Cryptocurrency Market

Emily Jacobs

Table of Contents

INTRODUCTION

Welcome to "Deciphering the Bitcoin Blueprint: Mastering Bitcoin - Strategies for Success in the Cryptocurrency Market." Bitcoin has been sweeping the globe in recent years, completely changing how we think about money, investing, and finance. Being the first virtual currency, Bitcoin has drawn interest from millions of people. It has made news for its sudden price increases and has attracted both supporters and detractors.

The decentralized ledger known as blockchain, which powers Bitcoin and many other cryptocurrencies and promises transparency, security, and immutability, is the driving force behind this technological marvel. Learning to use Bitcoin has become essential for anyone hoping to trade the cryptocurrency market successfully and confidently in the ever-changing world of digital currencies.

This book is intended to serve as your all-in-one resource, giving you the skills and information, you need to succeed in the volatile world of cryptocurrencies. Whether you are a beginner interested in Bitcoin's potential or an expert investor trying to hone your strategy, our goal is to arm you with the knowledge and resources you need to make wise choices and lay the groundwork for your cryptocurrency adventure.

We shall examine the foundations of Bitcoin, go into its past, and comprehend the workings of the larger cryptocurrency market throughout this book. You will discover the possible advantages and disadvantages of investing in Bitcoin and how to create a sound investment plan that complements your financial objectives.

Successful cryptocurrency trading requires a strong foundation in both technical and fundamental analysis. We'll walk you through the key methods for evaluating Bitcoin's long-term prospects and analyzing its price fluctuations. Additionally, we will provide advice and best practices to help you navigate the cryptocurrency market wisely, avoiding typical traps and seizing opportunities.

In the quickly changing world of digital assets, security is critical. As a result, we'll offer advice on how to keep your Bitcoin holdings safe, secure your wallets, and defend yourself from any potential dangers related to cryptocurrencies.

Lastly, we'll look closer at Bitcoin and cryptocurrencies' future, examining potential opportunities and difficulties. The landscape of digital finance is dynamic, and our mission is to provide you with the knowledge you need to keep up and prosper on this fascinating path.

As you delve through the pages of this book, keep in mind that the keys to success in the cryptocurrency market are knowledge and careful analysis. If you exercise diligence and caution, you may successfully traverse this fascinating frontier and use Bitcoin's potential to help you reach your financial objectives.

"Deciphering the Bitcoin Blueprint: Mastering Bitcoin - Strategies for Success in the Cryptocurrency Market" is a trustworthy guide for anyone interested in learning more about the fascinating realm of cryptocurrencies, be they a trader, investor, or just a curious observer.

Let's take this life-changing adventure together and discover the keys to succeeding in the cryptocurrency market. Let's get going!

CHAPTER I

Understanding Bitcoin Basics

What is Bitcoin: a decentralized digital currency

In recent years, a revolutionary force has emerged in finance and technology, reshaping how we perceive money and challenging the traditional notions of currency. At the forefront of this digital transformation stands Bitcoin, a decentralized digital currency that has captured the imagination of millions. Bitcoin debuted in 2009 when a mysterious individual or group functioning under a pseudonym of Satoshi Nakamoto released the now-famous Bitcoin whitepaper titled "Bitcoin: A Peer-to-Peer Electronic Cash System." This seminal document laid the foundation for an entirely new paradigm of currency that would operate independently of any central authority or intermediary.

Nakamoto's vision was to create a currency that would be free from the control of governments and financial institutions, putting the power of money back into the hands of the people. Bitcoin was to be a peer-to-peer electronic cash system, allowing individuals to conduct direct transactions with one another without the need for intermediaries like banks or payment processors. At the heart of Bitcoin's revolutionary design lies blockchain technology. A distributed ledger known as the blockchain safely, openly, and irrevocably logs every Bitcoin transaction ever made. This technology eliminates the need for a central authority to validate transactions, making it a decentralized and trustless system.

When a user starts a Bitcoin transaction, it is disseminated to a network of computers known as nodes. These nodes work together to verify the transaction's validity using complex cryptographic algorithms. Once validated, the transaction is combined with others into a block. Every block has a reference to the block before it, creating a chain of blocks - the blockchain. Miners are crucial in the Bitcoin network. They compete to solve complex mathematical puzzles, and the first one to solve the puzzle gets to add a new block to the blockchain. As a reward for their efforts, the winning miner receives newly minted Bitcoins and transaction fees from the included transactions. This process, known as mining, ensures the security and integrity of the Bitcoin network.

The decentralized nature of Bitcoin is one of its most distinctive characteristics. Bitcoin runs on a peer-to-peer network decentralized from a central authority, contrary to traditional currencies that are administered by governments and central banks. This decentralization has several key implications. Firstly, it means no single entity controls the Bitcoin network. No government or organization can arbitrarily manipulate the supply of Bitcoin or impose restrictions on its use. This has significant implications for financial sovereignty and personal freedoms, especially in regions with volatile economies or oppressive regimes.

Secondly, the decentralized nature of Bitcoin ensures a high level of security. Traditional financial systems are vulnerable to single points of failure, making them susceptible to hacking and fraud. In contrast, the Bitcoin network's distributed nature means there is no central point of vulnerability, making it more resistant to attacks. Furthermore, decentralization fosters inclusivity. The Bitcoin network is open to anybody with access to the internet, regardless of location, background, or financial situation. This accessibility can potentially empower the unbanked and underprivileged populations, providing them with access to financial services and opportunities previously unavailable to them.

In conclusion, Bitcoin represents a paradigm shift in finance and technology. Based on the ideas of blockchain technology, this decentralized digital currency gives people financial control and creates a more pleasant and secure financial environment. As Bitcoin continues to gain mainstream recognition and adoption, its impact on the global economy and financial landscape will likely be profound, challenging existing norms and paving the way for a more decentralized and equitable future.

How does Bitcoin work: blockchain technology explained

In the world of cryptocurrencies, Bitcoin stands tall as the pioneering digital currency that has captured the attention of millions around the globe. But how does Bitcoin work? What lies at the core of this revolutionary financial system? The answer lies in blockchain technology, the innovative backbone of Bitcoin and many other cryptocurrencies.

At its essence, a blockchain is a distributed and decentralized ledger that records transactions transparently and immutable. The term "blockchain" refers to how data is structured into blocks, each containing a list of transactions, and then linked together in chronological order, forming an unbroken chain. This innovative structure ensures that once a block is added to the chain, its data cannot be altered or tampered with, providing high security and integrity.

Blockchain differs from conventional centralized systems in that it is decentralized. A centralized system exposes the database to censorship, manipulation, and single points of failure because it is controlled by a single entity or authority. In contrast, a blockchain operates on a network of computers, known as nodes, each holding a copy of the entire blockchain. This decentralized distribution ensures that no single entity has the power to control or alter the data, enhancing transparency and trust.

The Bitcoin blockchain is the foundation for the entire Bitcoin network. When a user starts a Bitcoin transaction, it is disseminated to the network and grouped with other pending transactions into a "block." Each block contains a unique identifier known as a "hash," representing the data within the block. Additionally, each block includes the previous block's hash, effectively linking them together in chronological order.

The process of adding a new block to the blockchain is known as "mining." Miners are crucial in the Bitcoin network, and their task is to compete in solving complex mathematical puzzles. The first miner to find the solution for the puzzle gets the right to add the new block to the blockchain. This process is computationally intensive and requires substantial amounts of electricity, leading to the term "proof-of-work" (PoW) consensus mechanism.

Once a block is successfully mined and added to the blockchain, it becomes a permanent part of the historical record. Attempts to alter any data within the block would require changing the block's hash, which, in turn, would affect all of the following blocks in the chain. As each block is intrinsically linked to the one before it, any tampering with the data becomes virtually impossible due to the distributed nature of the blockchain.

The security and immutability of the blockchain are critical elements that enable trust in the Bitcoin network. The decentralized nature of the blockchain makes sure that no single entity can control the majority of nodes, preventing malicious actors from gaining control and manipulating the system. Additionally, the PoW consensus mechanism makes the blockchain resilient against attacks and ensures that all nodes in the network reach a consensus on the authenticity of transactions.

To participate in the Bitcoin network, users need a pair of cryptographic keys - a public and private keys. The public key is a unique identifier that serves as the user's address on the network. It is used to receive Bitcoin payments from others. On the other hand, the private key is a secret and cryptographically generated key that serves as the user's digital signature. It is employed to verify ownership of the Bitcoins linked to the relevant public key and to sign transactions.

The resilience of cryptographic algorithms is essential to the security of the Bitcoin network. Complex mathematical functions are used to generate both public and private keys, making it impossible for anyone to compute the private key from the public key. This cryptographic security provides a secure and tamper-resistant means of conducting transactions in the Bitcoin network.

In a decentralized network like Bitcoin, achieving consensus among all participants is crucial for maintaining the integrity of the blockchain. Consensus mechanisms make sure that each and every nodes in the network agree on the validity of transactions and the order in which they are recorded on the blockchain. Bitcoin primarily relies on the PoW consensus mechanism to achieve this agreement.

While PoW has effectively secured the Bitcoin network, it has some drawbacks. It requires significant computational power and consumes a substantial amount of electricity, leading to concerns about the environmental impact of Bitcoin mining. As a result, alternative consensus mechanisms, such as proof-of-stake (PoS) and delegated proof-of-stake (DPoS), have emerged, aiming to address these issues while maintaining the security and decentralization of the network.

As the popularity of Bitcoin and other cryptocurrencies has grown, so have concerns about the scalability of blockchain networks. The decentralized nature of blockchain, while providing security and transparency, also introduces scalability challenges. In the case of Bitcoin, the limited block size and the time required to mine a block create a bottleneck, restricting the number of transactions the network can handle per second.

Various solutions have been proposed to address these scalability challenges. The Lightning Network, a layer-two protocol constructed on top of the Bitcoin blockchain, is one such solution. By allowing users to establish payment channels with one another, the Lightning Network facilitates quicker and less expensive off-chain transactions. By reducing the number of on-chain transactions, the Lightning Network aims to alleviate congestion on the Bitcoin blockchain and increase its scalability.

Another approach is the development of second-layer blockchains or sidechains. These are separate blockchains that can interact with the main Bitcoin blockchain, allowing for faster and more efficient transactions. Sidechains can enable the development of specialized applications while benefiting from the security and decentralization of the leading Bitcoin network.

While Bitcoin remains the most prominent application of blockchain technology, its potential extends far beyond digital currencies. Blockchain can revolutionize various industries by introducing transparency, security, and efficiency.

One such industry is supply chain management. By utilizing blockchain to track the provenance of goods and verify their authenticity, companies can reduce counterfeiting and improve traceability. Additionally, blockchain-based smart contracts can automate and enforce the terms of agreements, streamlining business processes and reducing the need for intermediaries.

Another area where blockchain shows promise is in voting and identity verification. Blockchain-based voting systems can strengthen the integrity of elections by providing transparent and tamper-proof records. Moreover, blockchain-based identity solutions can empower individuals to securely control and share their personal data, mitigating concerns about data breaches and unauthorized access.

Blockchain is also making waves in decentralized finance (DeFi). DeFi platforms use smart contracts to provide financial services such as lending, borrowing, and trading without the need for traditional intermediaries. These platforms offer increased accessibility, reduced costs, and greater financial inclusivity.

In conclusion, blockchain technology is at the core of Bitcoin's revolutionary financial system. Through its decentralized and immutable nature, blockchain ensures the transparency and safety of the Bitcoin network, empowering users with control over their finances. As blockchain technology continues to evolve, it holds the potential to transform various industries, paving the way for a decentralized and trustless future. Whether in finance, supply chain management, voting, or identity verification, blockchain's transformative potential is boundless. As we embrace this innovative technology, we embark on a journey that challenges existing norms, fosters innovation, and redefines the future of our interconnected world.

Key terms and concepts: wallet, private keys, public keys, mining, etc.

In the rapidly evolving world of cryptocurrencies, understanding the fundamental terms and concepts is crucial for anyone looking to delve into this exciting and transformative realm. As digital assets gain mainstream recognition, terms like wallet, private keys, public keys, and mining become essential building blocks in comprehending the mechanics of cryptocurrencies.

A cryptocurrency wallet is a digital tool allowing users to store, send, as well as receive cryptocurrencies securely. Contrary to traditional wallets holding physical cash and cards, cryptocurrency wallets keep digital assets. These wallets utilize cryptographic keys, consisting of public and private keys, to interact with the blockchain network and facilitate transactions. There are several types of cryptocurrency wallets, each offering a different level of security and convenience.

At the heart of cryptocurrency wallets lie public keys and private keys. These cryptographic keys form the foundation of secure transactions and enable users to interact with the blockchain network. A public key is a special alphanumeric string generated from a user's private key. It serves as the wallet's address, allowing others to send cryptocurrencies to that specific address. Conversely, a private key is a long, randomly generated sequence of characters known only to the wallet owner. It acts as the password or secret key that grants access to the cryptocurrencies stored in the wallet.

Cryptocurrency mining is a crucial process that is central in maintaining the integrity and security of the blockchain network. It involves solving complex mathematical puzzles, known as Proof-of-Work (PoW) in the case of Bitcoin, to validate transactions and put them to the blockchain. Miners, individuals or entities partaking in the mining process, compete to solve these mathematical puzzles. The first miner to find the solution can add a new block to the blockchain. As a reward for their efforts, the miner receives newly minted cryptocurrencies and any transaction fees included in the block.

Consensus mechanisms are protocols used to achieve agreement among network participants on the validity of transactions and the order in which they are added to the blockchain. As blockchains operate in a decentralized manner, consensus mechanisms are essential to ensure that all nodes in the network reach agreement without the need for a central authority. Proof-of-Work (PoW), used by Bitcoin, relies on miners solving mathematical puzzles to validate transactions and secure the network. Other consensus mechanisms, such as Proof-of-Stake (or PoS) and Delegated Proof-of-Stake (or DPoS), offer alternative approaches to achieving consensus.

Smart contracts are automatically carrying out agreements that have the terms of the contract encoded directly into the code. These contracts operate on blockchain networks and, upon the fulfillment of certain requirements, automatically carry out predetermined activities. Smart contracts eliminate the requirement for intermediaries, such as lawyers or notaries, as the code enforces the agreement's terms transparently and impartially. They enable trustless interactions between parties, as the code ensures that all parties comply with the contract's conditions before any action is executed.

Decentralized Finance, or DeFi, is an emerging ecosystem that seeks to recreate traditional financial services using blockchain technology. DeFi protocols leverage smart contracts to offer services such as lending, borrowing, decentralized exchanges, stablecoins, and yield farming. Participants can lend their cryptocurrencies to earn interest, borrow funds against collateral, or trade assets directly without relying on centralized exchanges.

Privacy coins are a subcategory of cryptocurrencies that prioritize user privacy and anonymity. Unlike transparent blockchains like Bitcoin, where all transactions and addresses are visible to anyone, privacy coins use advanced cryptographic techniques to complicate transaction details and protect user identities. Monero and Zcash are two notable examples of privacy coins.

Tokenization is a process that entails converting real-world assets, like real estate, art, or commodities, into digital tokens on a blockchain. These tokens represent ownership or rights to the underlying asset, enabling fractional ownership and easy transferability. Tokenization offers several advantages, including increased liquidity, lower transaction costs, and enhanced accessibility to previously illiquid assets.

Central Bank Digital Currencies (CBDCs) are digital versions of a country's fiat currency, issued and regulated by its central bank. CBDCs aim to complement or replace physical cash, offering a digital representation of the national currency. CBDCs come in two main forms: retail CBDCs and wholesale CBDCs. Retail CBDCs are directly accessible to the public and can be used for everyday transactions like cash.

In conclusion, understanding key terms and concepts in the world of cryptocurrencies is essential for navigating this dynamic and transformative landscape. From wallets and cryptographic keys to mining, consensus mechanisms, smart contracts, DeFi, privacy coins, tokenization, and CBDCs, each element plays a crucial role in shaping blockchain networks' decentralized and trustless nature. As the crypto space evolves, staying informed and adapting to the latest developments will be vital for individuals looking to engage with cryptocurrencies and embrace their opportunities and innovations.

CHAPTER II

The History of Bitcoin

Origins of Bitcoin and its creator, Satoshi Nakamoto

The birth of Bitcoin in 2009 marked the beginning of a revolutionary era in finance and technology. A decentralized digital currency, Bitcoin promised to disrupt traditional financial systems, empower individuals with financial sovereignty, and introduce a novel way to conduct peer-to-peer transactions. However, despite its widespread adoption and global impact, the true identity of Bitcoin's creator, known by the pseudonym Satoshi Nakamoto, remains shrouded in mystery.

The story of Bitcoin traces back to the early 2000s when cryptographic enthusiasts and researchers explored the concept of creating a decentralized digital currency. They aimed to develop a system that eliminated the need for intermediaries, such as banks and governments, while ensuring secure and transparent transactions. This vision culminated in the release of the Bitcoin whitepaper in October 2008.

The whitepaper with the title of, "Bitcoin: A Peer-to-Peer Electronic Cash System," authored by Satoshi Nakamoto, outlined the principles for a revolutionary digital currency. It described a decentralized network that utilized cryptographic techniques to enable secure, transparent, and censorship-resistant transactions between users without needing a central authority. By combining various existing technologies and concepts, such as cryptographic hashing, proof-of-work consensus, and the blockchain data structure, Nakamoto proposed an innovative solution to the double-spending problem plaguing previous digital currency attempts.

Despite the Bitcoin whitepaper's profound impact and the first cryptocurrency's creation, Satoshi Nakamoto's identity remains a mystery. The name "Satoshi Nakamoto" is widely believed to be a pseudonym, and the true identity of the individual or group behind it remains unknown. Nakamoto communicated with the early Bitcoin community through online forums and email but eventually withdrew from public engagement in 2010. Since then, no verifiable evidence has surfaced to reveal the real identity of Satoshi Nakamoto.

Numerous theories and claims have emerged over the years, attributing the creation of Bitcoin to various individuals and groups. Some notable figures, including computer scientists, cryptographers, and entrepreneurs, have been named potential candidates, but none definitively confirmed as Nakamoto.

The enigma of Nakamoto's identity has led to widespread fascination and speculation within the cryptocurrency community and beyond. While some believe that Nakamoto's anonymity was a deliberate choice to protect privacy and avoid undue attention, others argue that it may have been to prevent legal or regulatory scrutiny. Regardless of the reason, Nakamoto's decision to remain anonymous has added an air of mystique to the origins of Bitcoin.

After the Bitcoin whitepaper's release, Nakamoto and a small group of early adopters began actively developing and promoting the cryptocurrency. On January 3, 2009, Nakamoto mined the first-ever block, referred to as the "genesis block" or "block 0," which contained the message "The Times 03/Jan/2009 Chancellor on brink of second bailout for banks." This message was a timestamped reference to a headline from The Times, a British newspaper, that emphasized the relevance of Bitcoin's launch during the global financial crisis of 2008.

The mining of the genesis block marked the official birth of the Bitcoin blockchain and the beginning of a new era in financial history. As Bitcoin gained traction and popularity, Nakamoto engaged with the early community, providing insights, clarifications, and technical support. However, Nakamoto's public presence diminished over time, and by mid-2010, all communications from Nakamoto ceased.

Despite Nakamoto's departure, the Bitcoin community continued to grow and evolve. Early adopters and enthusiasts, captivated by the concept of decentralized digital currency, rallied behind the development and promotion of Bitcoin. Over the years, developers, businesses, investors, and ordinary users contributed to the expansion of the cryptocurrency ecosystem.

Bitcoin's early years were marked by experimentation, volatility, and challenges. Nonetheless, the cryptocurrency's decentralized nature and censorship-resistant properties resonated with a growing audience seeking an alternative to traditional financial systems.

As Bitcoin approaches its second decade, its future remains subject to ongoing debates and uncertainties. The cryptocurrency continues to face challenges related to scalability, regulatory scrutiny, and evolving technologies. Furthermore, the international regulatory environment surrounding cryptocurrencies is still evolving, with several nations taking different approaches in addressing the potential benefits and risks associated with digital currencies.

Nonetheless, the core principles and potential of Bitcoin remain intact. Its decentralized nature, limited supply, and transparent blockchain have solidified its position as a store of value and a medium of exchange. As the technology evolves and innovative solutions emerge, Bitcoin's potential to transform financial systems and empower individuals with financial sovereignty continues to resonate with millions worldwide.

In conclusion, the origins of Bitcoin and its creator, Satoshi Nakamoto, stand as a testament to the power of technology and human ingenuity. From a concept presented in a whitepaper to a global phenomenon, Bitcoin's journey has been marked by challenges, controversies, and moments of triumph. While the identity of its creator remains shrouded in mystery, the impact of Bitcoin on the world of finance and technology is undeniable. As we look to the future, the continued evolution and adoption of Bitcoin will shape the digital currency revolution, redefining how we perceive and interact with money and financial systems.

Bitcoin's early adoption and challenges faced

The appearance of Bitcoin in 2009 marked the beginning of a new generation in finance and technology. As the first decentralized digital currency, Bitcoin promised to revolutionize how we perceive and interact with money. In its early days, the cryptocurrency faced numerous challenges, yet it also gained traction among a niche community of enthusiasts.

Bitcoin was born from the vision of its anonymous creator, Satoshi Nakamoto, who introduced the concept of a peer-to-peer electronic cash system in the Bitcoin whitepaper published in October 2008. The whitepaper laid the foundation for a decentralized network that allowed individuals to transact directly with one another without the need for intermediaries like banks or financial institutions. By combining cryptographic techniques and a transparent public ledger known as the blockchain, Nakamoto aimed to address the double-spending problem plaguing previous digital currency attempts.

Bitcoin's early days were characterized by a small and passionate community of individuals who shared a belief in its transformative potential. The early adopters, commonly referred to as "Bitcoin pioneers," were predominantly technologists, cryptographers, and libertarian-minded individuals who saw the promise of a financial system free from central control and censorship in Bitcoin. In the first few years after its launch, Bitcoin gained popularity primarily within online communities and forums dedicated to cryptography, cypherpunk ideals, and digital currencies.

Mining, the process of confirming transactions and adding them to the blockchain, played a crucial role in the early adoption of Bitcoin. In the initial days, mining could be done using standard personal computers, and early adopters were able to acquire significant amounts of Bitcoin through mining with relatively little competition. The early transactions involving Bitcoin were modest in value, with users experimenting with the digital currency for various purposes. Some engaged in small trades and purchases to test the functionality, while others simply held onto their Bitcoins as an investment, believing in its long-term potential.

One of the most celebrated milestones in Bitcoin's early adoption was the infamous "Bitcoin Pizza Day." A programmer by the name of Laszlo Hanyecz made a history on May 22, 2010, when he paid two pizzas for 10,000 Bitcoins. This transaction amounted to approximately $41, marking the first known commercial transaction involving Bitcoin. Given that the 10,000 Bitcoins would now be valued millions of dollars, Bitcoin Pizza Day serves as a bittersweet reminder of the remarkable growth in value of cryptocurrencies. Bitcoin Pizza Day exemplifies the willingness of early adopters to use their digital currency for real-world transactions, even in its infancy when its value was still uncertain and relatively low.

As Bitcoin gained traction, it encountered several growing pains, primarily related to scalability and user experience. The Bitcoin blockchain's limited block size and processing capacity became apparent bottlenecks, leading to delays in transaction confirmations and increased fees during periods of high demand. These scalability issues were exacerbated as the Bitcoin network's user base expanded. As more people began using Bitcoin, the network experienced congestion, resulting in slower transaction processing times and higher fees. The user experience of early Bitcoin wallets and exchanges also presented challenges. Early Bitcoin wallets were often complex and difficult to use for non-technical users, making the onboarding process cumbersome. Similarly, early Bitcoin exchanges were susceptible to hacking and lacked the robust security measures seen in modern cryptocurrency exchanges.

Another major hurdle to Bitcoin's early adoption was the issue of security and trust. As a new and untested technology, Bitcoin faced skepticism and criticism, with some questioning the security of the network and the potential for fraudulent activities. One significant event that impacted trust in Bitcoin's early days was hacking the Mt. Gox exchange in 2011. Mt. Gox, one of the earliest and most prominent Bitcoin exchanges at the time, suffered a series of breaches in security that led to the loss of thousands of Bitcoins belonging to its users. This incident highlighted the vulnerability of early exchanges and underscored the importance of secure storage solutions for cryptocurrencies.

Bitcoin's decentralized nature and global reach raised regulatory challenges in various jurisdictions. In the early days of cryptocurrency, many governments struggled to categorize and regulate Bitcoin, unsure of how to apply existing financial regulations to this new and innovative technology. The lack of clear regulations and the potential for illicit use created uncertainties for businesses and individuals looking to engage with Bitcoin. The regulatory landscape continued to evolve, and some countries embraced cryptocurrencies more openly, while others took a more cautious approach, imposing restrictions or outright bans on Bitcoin-related activities.

Despite its challenges, Bitcoin's early adoption was a crucial period in the cryptocurrency's development. The passion and dedication of its early adopters laid the foundation for a growing community that continues to embrace and advance Bitcoin's vision today. Overcoming scalability issues and security concerns, the Bitcoin network evolved and improved, facilitating faster and more secure transactions. User experience also saw significant enhancements, with the development of user-friendly wallets and exchanges that catered to a broader audience. Bitcoin's early adoption was marked by milestones such as the first commercial transaction, forming a passionate community, and increased media attention. While challenges remain, these early triumphs served as a testament to the potential of this revolutionary digital currency.

In conclusion, Bitcoin's early adoption was a period of exploration, experimentation, and growth. The cryptocurrency's ability to overcome challenges and garner support from a passionate community propelled it from an obscure concept to a global phenomenon. As Bitcoin continues to mature and gain acceptance, its early days will be remembered as a pivotal moment in the history of finance and technology, setting the stage for a decentralized future.

Milestones and significant events in Bitcoin's history

Since its inception in 2009, Bitcoin has gone through a remarkable journey, transforming from a niche experimental project to a global financial phenomenon. Over the years, several key milestones and significant events have shaped the trajectory of Bitcoin's history, driving its adoption, technological advancements, and regulatory developments.

The journey of Bitcoin began on January 3, 2009, when its mysterious creator, Satoshi Nakamoto, mined the first-ever block, also known as the "genesis block" or "block 0." The block contained the message "The Times 03/Jan/2009 Chancellor on brink of second bailout for banks," referencing Bitcoin's vision as an alternative to the traditional financial system during the global financial crisis of 2008. The mining of the genesis block marked the official start of the Bitcoin blockchain and set the stage for a decentralized and censorship-resistant digital currency.

Bitcoin experienced modest adoption in its early days, primarily within cryptography and cypherpunk communities. The first notable milestone was the "Bitcoin Pizza Day" on May 22, 2010, when Laszlo Hanyecz made history by purchasing two pizzas for 10,000 Bitcoins. This transaction amounted to about $41 at the time, but today, those 10,000 Bitcoins would be worth millions of dollars. This event underscored the potential value and utility of Bitcoin as a medium of exchange.

Another noteworthy achievement was when Bitcoin's price broke $1 for the first time in 2011, signaling a considerable rise in value since the platform's founding. Subsequent price milestones further fueled interest in the cryptocurrency, drawing attention from media and investors alike.

Mt. Gox, founded in 2010 by Jed McCaleb, was the first major Bitcoin exchange and quickly became the largest, handling over 70% of Bitcoin transactions at its peak. Its growth played a vital role in driving Bitcoin's early adoption, but it also faced numerous challenges. In 2014, Mt. Gox suspended withdrawals, citing a technical glitch. However, it was later revealed that the exchange had lost approximately 850,000 Bitcoins due to a long-term hacking attack, leading to bankruptcy. This event, known as the "Mt. Gox incident," was a turning point for the cryptocurrency industry, exposing the need for robust security measures and regulatory oversight.

One of the fundamental aspects of Bitcoin is its fixed supply of 21 million coins, making it deflationary by nature. A halving event occurs every 210,000 blocks, or approximately every four years, reducing the block reward miners receive by half. The first halving happened in November 2012, mitigating the block reward from 50 down to 25 Bitcoins. The second halving occurred in July 2016, decreasing the block reward to 12.5 Bitcoins. These halvings have contributed to Bitcoin's scarcity, driving its value and increasing its appeal as a store of value.

In 2011, the darknet marketplace Silk Road was launched by Ross Ulbricht, providing a platform for anonymous transactions using Bitcoin. The marketplace primarily facilitated the buying and selling of illegal goods and services, leading to significant media attention and regulatory concerns about Bitcoin's association with illicit activities. In 2013, the FBI shut down Silk Road and arrested Ulbricht, leading to the auction of over 144,000 seized Bitcoins. The Silk Road incident further highlighted the need for a balanced approach to regulating cryptocurrencies, recognizing their potential benefits and risks.

While Bitcoin was the first cryptocurrency, Ethereum, created by Vitalik Buterin and launched in 2015, introduced a groundbreaking innovation known as smart contracts. Decentralized apps and programmable transactions on the blockchain are made possible by smart contracts, which are essentially self-executing contracts with conditions explicitly encoded into code. Ethereum's launch marked the rise of blockchain platforms beyond cryptocurrencies, inspiring the development of a vast ecosystem of decentralized applications and new use cases. The advent of Ethereum also opened doors for Initial Coin Offerings (ICOs), allowing projects to raise funds by issuing their native tokens on the Ethereum blockchain.

As Bitcoin gained popularity, it faced a critical challenge regarding its scalability. The limited block size of 1 MB created a bottleneck, causing delays in transaction confirmations and higher fees during periods of high demand. This issue sparked a contentious debate within the community about how best to scale the Bitcoin network. The discussion primarily revolved around two competing solutions: increasing the block size (Bitcoin Cash) and implementing a second-layer scaling solution called the Lightning Network. The disagreement led to a "hard fork" in August 2017, creating Bitcoin Cash. The scaling debate highlighted the challenges of achieving consensus in decentralized communities and the complexities of making protocol changes in a secure and decentralized manner.

The growing interest from institutional investors and traditional financial institutions has been a significant milestone for Bitcoin. In December 2017, Bitcoin reached a record-high price of nearly $20,000, primarily driven by retail investors' enthusiasm. Following the bull run, several large financial institutions expressed interest in the cryptocurrency. Institutional investors can now speculate on Bitcoin's price swings thanks to the December 2017 launch of Bitcoin futures contracts by Chicago Mercantile Exchange (CME) and Chicago Board Options Exchange (CBOE). This marked a notable moment of mainstream recognition for Bitcoin and facilitated greater institutional participation in the cryptocurrency market.

Bitcoin's global impact has prompted governments worldwide to address its regulation. Different countries have adopted various approaches, ranging from outright bans to embracing cryptocurrencies and blockchain technology. Japan, for instance, recognized Bitcoin as legal tender in 2017, leading to a surge in adoption and acceptance. In the United States, regulatory bodies like the Securities and Exchange Commission (SEC) have guided cryptocurrency regulations, focusing on investor protection and combating fraud. Regulatory clarity remains a critical milestone for the cryptocurrency industry, enabling legitimate businesses to thrive while safeguarding users' interests.

As Bitcoin's popularity surged, concerns about its energy consumption and environmental impact also grew. Bitcoin mining, a process that validates transactions and secures the network, requires substantial computing power, leading to significant electricity consumption, predominantly from fossil fuels in some regions. The environmental impact of Bitcoin has sparked debates and prompted discussions about sustainable mining practices and the need for more energy-efficient consensus mechanisms. As a result, some mining operations have sought to utilize renewable energy sources to mitigate the cryptocurrency's carbon footprint.

In conclusion, Bitcoin's history has been characterized by a series of milestones and significant events that have shaped its evolution and impact on the global financial landscape. From its humble beginnings with mining the genesis block to its widespread adoption and acceptance by institutions, Bitcoin's journey has been remarkable and transformative. While it has faced challenges such as scalability and regulatory scrutiny, Bitcoin has demonstrated resilience and an enduring appeal as a decentralized store of value and a borderless means of exchange. As it continues to evolve, its milestones will undoubtedly shape the future of cryptocurrencies and blockchain technology, leaving a lasting legacy in the annals of financial history. The story of Bitcoin is far from over, as it continues to inspire innovation and disrupt traditional financial systems, setting the stage for a decentralized future.

CHAPTER III

Analyzing the Current Cryptocurrency Market

Overview of the broader cryptocurrency market

The rise of Bitcoin in 2009 marked the beginning of a new era in finance, with cryptocurrencies emerging as a disruptive force challenging traditional financial systems. Over the years, the cryptocurrency market has evolved and expanded, encompassing a vast array of digital assets beyond Bitcoin. As of the time of writing, thousands of cryptocurrencies exist, each with unique features and use cases. Ethereum, launched in 2015, is one of the most prominent altcoins and has contributed significantly to the expansion of the cryptocurrency market by introducing smart contract functionality.

Other cryptocurrencies have also gained traction in specific niches, such as Ripple (XRP) for cross-border payments, Litecoin (LTC) for faster transactions, and Cardano (ADA) for its focus on sustainability and scalability. The diversity of cryptocurrencies reflects the wide range of applications and innovations that blockchain technology has enabled.

The cryptocurrency market's growth is evident in its total market capitalization, which refers to the combined value of all cryptocurrencies in circulation. As the first and most well-known cryptocurrency, Bitcoin has historically held the largest market capitalization, often accounting for a significant percentage of the total market cap.

However, as the broader cryptocurrency market has expanded, Bitcoin's dominance has gradually decreased. While it remains the most significant individual cryptocurrency by market capitalization, its overall market share has reduced as investors explore other cryptocurrencies with different use cases and growth potential.

The cryptocurrency market is known for its high volatility, with prices subject to rapid and substantial fluctuations. Market sentiment, regulatory developments, technological advancements, and macroeconomic factors influence cryptocurrency prices. As a result, the market is often characterized by bull and bear cycles, with periods of rapid price appreciation followed by significant corrections.

The cryptocurrency market's volatility presents both opportunities and challenges for investors and traders. On the other hand, it can lead to substantial gains for those who time their investments well. On the other hand, it also poses risks for investors, as prices can quickly reverse, leading to potential losses.

Cryptocurrency exchanges play a crucial role in facilitating the buying and selling of digital assets. These platforms provide a marketplace where users can exchange cryptocurrencies for fiat currencies (e.g., USD, EUR) or other cryptocurrencies. Exchanges vary regarding the number of supported cryptocurrencies, trading volumes, and security measures.

Some exchanges are centralized, meaning a single entity operates them, while others are decentralized, relying on blockchain technology and smart contracts to allow peer-to-peer trading without an intermediary. The choice of exchange can impact the ease of trading, liquidity, and security of an individual's cryptocurrency holdings.

The cryptocurrency market's decentralized and borderless nature has presented challenges for regulators worldwide. Governments have grappled with the classification of cryptocurrencies and how to apply existing financial regulations to this new asset class. The lack of uniformity in regulations across different jurisdictions has created uncertainty for market participants and businesses operating in the cryptocurrency space.

Concerns including terrorist financing, money laundering, and consumer protection have also raised concerns for regulators. As a result, some countries have imposed strict regulations or outright bans on cryptocurrency-related activities, while others have taken a more proactive approach, seeking to foster innovation while ensuring investor protection.

Recent years have seen a sharp growth in institutional interest in cryptocurrencies, which has led to higher adoption and investment levels. Major financial institutions, hedge funds, and asset management companies have started including cryptocurrencies in their investment portfolios. Some institutional investors view cryptocurrencies as a hedge against inflation and traditional market risks, while others see them as a potential source of high returns.

Additionally, several publicly traded companies have added Bitcoin to their corporate treasuries, signaling a shift in the perception of cryptocurrencies from speculative assets to legitimate stores of value.

Mainstream adoption of cryptocurrencies has also been boosted by integrating digital assets into various payment systems and financial products. Payment processors and fintech companies have introduced cryptocurrency payment options, allowing users to use cryptocurrencies for everyday purchases. Furthermore, the development of cryptocurrency-backed financial products, such as exchange-traded funds (ETFs) and futures contracts, has made it easier for traditional investors to acquire exposure to the cryptocurrency market.

The evolution of the cryptocurrency market has given rise to innovative applications beyond simple digital currencies. Decentralized Finance, or DeFi has emerged as a prominent use case, offering a range of financial services built on blockchain technology. DeFi platforms enable users to access lending, borrowing, and trading services without intermediaries, fostering financial inclusion and accessibility.

Non-fungible tokens (NFTs) have also garnered significant attention, representing unique digital assets tied to specific items, artwork, or digital content. NFTs have enabled artists, musicians, and content creators to tokenize and monetize their work in a new and decentralized manner, creating new opportunities for ownership and revenue generation.

The energy-intensive nature of cryptocurrency mining, particularly for proof-of-work-based blockchains like Bitcoin, has raised environmental concerns. Critics argue that the substantial electricity consumption associated with mining contributes to carbon emissions and exacerbates climate change.

In response, some cryptocurrency projects have sought to address environmental concerns by exploring alternative consensus mechanisms, such as proof-of-stake, which requires significantly less energy. Additionally, initiatives have been launched to encourage the utilization of renewable energy sources for mining operations, aiming to mitigate the carbon footprint of the cryptocurrency industry.

In conclusion, the broader cryptocurrency market continues to be a dynamic and rapidly evolving landscape. The market has witnessed significant growth and diversification from its origins with Bitcoin to the proliferation of altcoins and the rise of DeFi and NFTs. Institutional involvement and mainstream adoption have further propelled cryptocurrencies into the spotlight, raising questions about their role in the future of finance.

However, the market also faces challenges, such as regulatory uncertainty, volatility, and environmental concerns. As the cryptocurrency market matures, finding a balance between innovation, investor protection, and environmental sustainability will be essential.

Overall, the cryptocurrency market remains a space of immense potential and disruption, where technological advancements and innovative use cases continue to shape its future. Whether it becomes a mainstream financial asset class or a complementary system to traditional finance, cryptocurrencies have undoubtedly left an indelible mark on the financial landscape, sparking a paradigm shift in how we perceive and interact with money and value.

Bitcoin's dominance and market trends

Bitcoin, the world's first cryptocurrency, has revolutionized the financial landscape and become a significant driving force in shaping the broader cryptocurrency market. Since its appearance in 2009, Bitcoin has experienced remarkable growth and has dominated the market for most of its history. In its early years, Bitcoin enjoyed a near-monopoly in the cryptocurrency space, holding the lion's share of the market capitalization. However, as the market matured and new cryptocurrencies emerged, Bitcoin's dominance declined slowly. Ethereum, launched in 2015, introduced smart contracts and opened the door to a vast ecosystem of decentralized applications (dApps) and innovative blockchain projects. This led to the rise of altcoins and marked the beginning of a diversification process within the cryptocurrency market.

Over the years, the proliferation of altcoins has chipped away at Bitcoin's dominance, but it remains the most significant individual cryptocurrency by market capitalization. As of the time of writing, Bitcoin's dominance hovers around 40%-50% of the total market capitalization of all cryptocurrencies. Despite the emergence of numerous altcoins, Bitcoin's unique value proposition as "digital gold" and a store of value has kept it at the forefront of the market. The narrative of scarcity, reinforced by its fixed supply of 21 million coins and periodic halving events that reduce the block reward, has attracted institutional investors seeking a hedge against inflation and traditional market risks.

Distinct market trends over time have characterized the cryptocurrency market. Notably, it has seen several cycles of bull and bear markets. During bull markets, cryptocurrencies experience substantial price appreciation, accompanied by heightened investor interest and positive market sentiment. The 2017 bull run is a notable example, during which Bitcoin's price surged to an all-time high, reaching nearly $20,000. This period saw widespread media coverage and a surge in interest from retail investors, leading to a broader market rally as many altcoins also experienced exponential price increases.

However, the euphoria of the 2017 bull run was followed by a protracted bear market, as prices underwent a significant correction. The cryptocurrency market experienced a prolonged period of decline and consolidation, leading to a more cautious approach from investors and a more critical assessment of the value propositions of different cryptocurrencies.

Various factors, including technological developments, regulatory changes, macroeconomic events, and investor sentiment influence the market trends in the cryptocurrency space. Technological advancements are crucial in driving market trends. Projects introducing novel solutions, such as improved scalability, enhanced privacy features, or interoperability between blockchains, tend to gain attention and attract investment. Moreover, regulatory developments impact market sentiment and influence investor behavior. Positive regulatory measures that foster innovation and provide clarity for businesses running in the cryptocurrency space can boost market confidence and attract institutional investment.

Institutional involvement has become a significant catalyst for market trends. Large financial institutions, hedge funds, and asset management companies have recognized the potential of cryptocurrencies as an asset class. Some view Bitcoin as a digital store of value and a hedge against economic uncertainties, similar to gold, while others see the potential for high returns in the broader cryptocurrency market. Institutional investment has brought greater liquidity and stability to the market, and traditional financial institutions' growing acceptance of cryptocurrencies has expanded their appeal to a broader audience.

The evolving dynamics of the cryptocurrency market present both challenges and opportunities. The high market volatility can lead to significant gains for investors who time their trades well, but it also poses risks for those who do not manage risk appropriately. Regulatory uncertainty stays a significant challenge for the industry as different countries adopt varying approaches to cryptocurrency regulation. Regulation clarity is essential to provide market participants with a stable and predictable environment.

The future of Bitcoin's dominance and market trends in cryptocurrency is difficult to predict with certainty. While Bitcoin has endured as the dominant cryptocurrency for over a decade, the landscape continually evolves. New technologies, innovative use cases, and changing market dynamics could lead to shifts in the balance of power among cryptocurrencies. Nevertheless, Bitcoin's role as the pioneering digital currency and its entrenched position in the market makes it a central player in the ongoing evolution of the broader cryptocurrency market.

In conclusion, Bitcoin's dominance and market trends have been shaped by its unique value proposition, its status as the first and most well-known cryptocurrency, and the emergence of altcoins that have sought to address different use cases and challenges in the blockchain space. As the cryptocurrency market matures, it has experienced bull and bear market cycles, driven by technological advancements, regulatory developments, investor sentiment, and institutional involvement. While Bitcoin's dominance has diminished over time due to the proliferation of altcoins, it remains a dominant force in the market and continues to be a key driver of innovation and adoption. The dynamic character of the cryptocurrency market offers both challenges and opportunities, and as it continues to evolve, it will shape the future of finance and the broader digital economy.

Market analysis tools and resources

The cryptocurrency market is a dynamic and fast-paced ecosystem, subject to significant price fluctuations and market sentiment swings. As the industry evolves, market participants seek to make informed decisions based on data-driven analysis. In this section, we will explore various market analysis tools and resources available to investors, traders, and enthusiasts in the cryptocurrency market. These tools are crucial in understanding market trends, identifying potential opportunities, and managing risks.

Price charts are fundamental tools traders and analysts use to visualize historical price movements of cryptocurrencies. Technical analysis involves interpreting these price charts to identify patterns, trends, and potential price reversals. Common chart patterns include "head and shoulders," "double tops," and "flags," among others. Technical indicators, like Relative Strength Index (or RSI), moving averages, and Bollinger Bands, provide additional insights into market momentum, the overbought or oversold conditions, and potential price targets. Price charts and technical analysis are valuable resources for traders looking to time their entry and exit points in the market.

Fundamental analysis concentrates on evaluating the intrinsic value of cryptocurrencies based on various factors, including the project's technology, use case, team, partnerships, and market adoption. Fundamental analysts evaluate whitepapers, development progress, community engagement, and the overall value proposition of a cryptocurrency. This analysis helps investors identify projects with long-term potential and distinguish between viable projects and those with questionable fundamentals.

Market sentiment indicators provide insights into the overall sentiment of market participants, indicating whether they are bullish (positive) or bearish (negative) about the market's future direction. Social media sentiment analysis, for example, uses natural language processing and also machine learning algorithms to analyze social media posts and gauge the overall sentiment toward a particular cryptocurrency. News sentiment analysis also tracks media coverage to assess whether news articles are positive, negative, or neutral, impacting market sentiment.

Cryptocurrency screeners allow users to filter and sort cryptocurrencies based on various parameters, such as price, market capitalization, trading volume, and percentage change. These screeners help investors and traders quickly identify cryptocurrencies that meet their specific criteria, facilitating efficient market analysis and research.

Cryptocurrency market heatmaps visually represent price movements for multiple cryptocurrencies simultaneously. They use color-coded cells to show the price change of each cryptocurrency relative to others over a specified period. Market heatmaps enable users to quickly spot trending cryptocurrencies or those experiencing significant price movements in real-time.

On-chain analytics tools leverage blockchain data to analyze network activity, transactions, and addresses. These tools offer insights into metrics like transaction volume, active addresses, transaction fees, and token distribution. On-chain analytics help users gauge the level of network activity and monitor potential whale movements or accumulation by significant holders.

Sentiment analysis tools assess market sentiment through text data from sources including news articles, social media posts, and forum discussions. By analyzing the language and context of discussions, sentiment analysis tools determine whether the overall sentiment is positive, negative, or neutral. This information helps traders and investors gauge market sentiment and make informed decisions.

Staying updated with the most current news and developments is crucial in the fast-paced cryptocurrency market. Market news aggregators collect and curate news articles, blog posts, and announcements from various sources, providing users with a extensive overview of the most relevant news impacting the market.

Coin metrics platforms offer comprehensive data on cryptocurrencies, including historical and real-time price data, trading volume, market capitalization, and liquidity metrics. Data providers ensure the accuracy and reliability of data, providing users with the necessary information to conduct thorough market analysis.

Cryptocurrency communities on platforms like Reddit, Telegram, and Discord are valuable resources for gathering insights and engaging with like-minded enthusiasts. These communities often discuss market trends, project updates, and potential investment opportunities.

Cryptocurrency exchanges offer real-time data on order books, displaying the buy and sell orders at various price levels. Traders use this data to assess market liquidity and potential support and resistance levels.

Several websites and research firms publish market analysis reports on cryptocurrencies and the broader market. These reports often provide in-depth analysis, market insights, and trend predictions, helping investors make informed decisions.

Trading platforms and application programming interfaces (APIs) provide access to real-time and historical market data and the ability to execute trades programmatically. These tools are essential for algorithmic trading strategies and automated trading bots.

In conclusion, the cryptocurrency market offers many market analysis tools and resources to assist investors, traders, and enthusiasts make informed decisions. From price charts and technical analysis to on-chain analytics, sentiment analysis, and fundamental research, these tools provide valuable insights into market trends, sentiment, and potential investment opportunities. As the cryptocurrency market evolves, the use of data-driven analysis and research becomes increasingly essential for navigating the dynamic and fast-paced ecosystem effectively. By leveraging these tools, market participants can enhance their understanding of the cryptocurrency market and make more informed decisions in this ever-changing landscape.

CHAPTER IV

The Benefits and Risks of Investing in Bitcoin

Potential benefits of investing in Bitcoin

Bitcoin, the world's first cryptocurrency, has captured the attention of investors worldwide since its inception in 2009. Over the years, it has evolved from a niche digital asset to a recognized store of value and a potential hedge against traditional market risks. One of the main benefits of investing in Bitcoin is its role as a store of value. Bitcoin's limited supply, with a fixed maximum of 21 million coins, makes it deflationary in nature. Because of its scarcity, Bitcoin's value is guaranteed not to decrease over time, in contrast to fiat currencies that may experience inflation as a result of central bank policy. As a result, like conventional safe-haven assets like gold, some investors see Bitcoin as a possible hedge against inflation and economic volatility.

Bitcoin's decentralized nature, operating on a peer-to-peer network without the need for intermediaries like banks, gives individuals more control over their finances. Users can send as well as receive Bitcoin directly without relying on third-party institutions, providing a sense of financial autonomy and reducing the risk of censorship or government intervention in financial transactions. This feature has particular appeal in regions with limited access to traditional banking services or countries with restrictive financial regulations.

Another significant benefit of investing in Bitcoin is the potential for high returns. Bitcoin's price history demonstrates significant potential for price appreciation over short periods. Investors who entered the market during its early stages saw astronomical returns as the price surged from mere cents to thousands of dollars. Although past performance does not indicate future results, the potential for high returns continues to attract speculative investors seeking to capitalize on market volatility.

Investing in Bitcoin can also offer portfolio diversification benefits, particularly for traditional investors seeking to expand their holdings beyond conventional assets like stocks and bonds. Cryptocurrencies, including Bitcoin, often exhibit low correlations with traditional asset classes. As a result, incorporating Bitcoin into an investment portfolio can help mitigate overall portfolio risk and increase potential returns during economic and market uncertainty periods.

Bitcoin's global accessibility allows anyone with an access on the internet to participate in the cryptocurrency market, regardless of geographical location or economic status. This inclusivity has the potential to provide financial opportunities to unbanked and underbanked populations worldwide. Bitcoin serves as a borderless and permissionless financial system, enabling financial inclusion for millions of individuals who lack access to traditional banking services.

Bitcoin has emerged as a viable alternative store of value in countries facing economic turmoil or hyperinflation. Citizens in such countries often face the devaluation of their local currencies, leading to a loss of purchasing power and economic instability. Bitcoin's global and decentralized nature provides a potential refuge for individuals seeking to preserve their wealth and escape the risks of unstable national currencies.

The increasing acceptance of Bitcoin among institutional investors and large corporations has brought legitimacy and credibility to the cryptocurrency market. Several major financial institutions, hedge funds, and asset management companies have allocated portions of their portfolios to Bitcoin. Publicly traded companies have also added Bitcoin to their corporate treasuries as a store of value. The increased institutional interest in Bitcoin has contributed to its broader acceptance in the mainstream financial industry.

Technological innovation and network security are also potential benefits of investing in Bitcoin. Bitcoin operates on a robust, secure blockchain network that relies on advanced cryptographic techniques. The underlying technology, known as blockchain, ensures the immutability of transaction records and the integrity of the network. As one of the first use cases of blockchain technology, Bitcoin has paved the way for further innovations and developments in the broader cryptocurrency and blockchain space.

Bitcoin's borderless nature allows for fast and low-cost cross-border transactions, making it an attractive choice for international remittances. Traditional remittance services are often associated with high fees and delays, especially for transactions between different countries and currencies. Bitcoin's decentralized system enables near-instant and cost-effective transfers, potentially benefiting millions of people who rely on remittances as a crucial source of income.

As one of the earliest cryptocurrencies, Bitcoin has established itself as a pioneer and standard-bearer for the broader cryptocurrency market. Its early adoption and widespread recognition have given it an advantage over many newer cryptocurrencies in terms of liquidity, market acceptance, and infrastructure development. Bitcoin's market maturity and established ecosystem contribute to its appeal for investors seeking a stable and well-established investment option in the cryptocurrency space.

In conclusion, investing in Bitcoin offers various potential benefits, making it an attractive option for diverse investors. Its status as a store of value, potential hedge against inflation, and unique characteristics as a decentralized and borderless digital asset have led to its widespread adoption and recognition. However, it is essential to take into account the inherent risks associated with the cryptocurrency market, including price volatility, regulatory uncertainties, and potential technological challenges. As with any investment, thorough research, risk management, and a long-term perspective are critical for making informed decisions and realizing the potential benefits of investing in Bitcoin.

Risks and challenges of Bitcoin investing

The first cryptocurrency, Bitcoin, has attracted a lot of interest from investors looking to diversify their holdings and profit from the possibility of large returns. It's important to be aware of the risks and difficulties involved with investing in Bitcoin, despite the fact that its special qualities and future rewards make it a desirable financial choice. The volatility of Bitcoin's price is one of the most notable concerns. In a short amount of time, the price of Bitcoin can fluctuate significantly, giving investors the opportunity to make large profits or losses. Volatility can offer traders profitable opportunities, but it can also result in unanticipated losses for those who do not properly manage risk. Investors should avoid making larger investments than they are prepared to lose and be ready for unexpected market fluctuations.

In the cryptocurrency industry, regulatory uncertainty is a significant risk as well. The regulatory environment surrounding cryptocurrencies is always changing, with numerous countries implementing various strategies. Governments and regulatory authorities may introduce new laws, restrictions, or taxation policies that can impact the cryptocurrency market. Regulation changes can create uncertainty and affect investor sentiment, potentially leading to price volatility. Investors must stay informed about regulatory developments and assess the potential impact on their investments.

Security risks are a critical concern when investing in Bitcoin. Securing Bitcoin holdings is crucial due to the irreversible nature of blockchain transactions. Investors who hold their own private keys are responsible for the security of their funds. Cybersecurity threats, such as hacking attacks, phishing attempts, and malware, pose significant risks to Bitcoin holders. To mitigate security risks, investors are advised to use reputable wallets and employ robust security practices, such as two-factor authentication and hardware wallets.

The cryptocurrency market is vulnerable to manipulation since it is smaller than traditional financial markets. Whales, individuals or entities holding significant amounts of Bitcoin, can influence the market by executing large buy or sell orders. Moreover, pump-and-dump schemes orchestrated by malicious actors can artificially inflate or deflate Bitcoin's price, leading to losses for unsuspecting investors. Investors must exercise caution and refrain from making decisions based on short-term price movements that may result from market manipulation.

Technological risks are also present in the cryptocurrency market. Bitcoin's underlying technology, blockchain, is still relatively new and subject to ongoing development. While blockchain has demonstrated robustness and security, it is not immune to technical issues, bugs, or vulnerabilities. In the past, software bugs and protocol upgrades have resulted in temporary network disruptions and forks, creating uncertainties for investors and traders. Investors should know potential technical risks and stay informed about any planned upgrades or changes to the Bitcoin network.

The lack of regulation and investor protection is another significant challenge in the cryptocurrency market. Because Bitcoin and other cryptocurrencies are decentralized, they function outside of the established financial system and are not as regulated or protected from investors as other cryptocurrencies. Bitcoin investments do not have the same recourse in cases involving fraud, theft, or disputes as traditional financial assets like stocks or bonds. Investors must exercise due diligence and be cautious when engaging with unregulated platforms or services in the cryptocurrency space.

The adoption and acceptance of Bitcoin are crucial factors that can impact its long-term value. While Bitcoin has seen increased adoption over the years, there is still uncertainty regarding its future acceptance as a mainstream currency or store of value. Negative sentiment, lack of use cases, or technological limitations could hinder widespread adoption, impacting the asset's long-term value.

Bitcoin investing can be emotionally challenging, especially during periods of extreme price volatility. The fear of missing out, often called FOMO, can result in impulsive decisions to invest at the peak of a price rally, while the fear of missing out (FOMO) can prompt panic selling during market downturns. Emotional reactions to market movements can cloud judgment and lead to irrational investment decisions. Investors must adopt a disciplined and rational approach to managing their investments.

Environmental concerns are also relevant in Bitcoin investing. Bitcoin mining, the process by which new Bitcoins are generated and transactions are verified, requires significant computational power and energy consumption. Critics have escalated concerns regarding the impact of Bitcoin mining on the environment, mainly when powered by fossil fuels. Environmental considerations may lead to increased scrutiny and calls for more sustainable mining practices, potentially affecting the mining landscape and investor sentiment.

In conclusion, while Bitcoin investing offers the potential for significant returns and portfolio diversification, it is essential to determine and manage the inherent risks and challenges associated with this digital asset. Price volatility, regulatory uncertainty, security risks, market manipulation, technological issues, lack of investor protections, adoption concerns, psychological risks, and environmental considerations are among the key factors investors must consider. A prudent approach involves conducting thorough research, understanding the underlying technology, and establishing a risk management strategy. By being aware of these risks and maintaining a long-term investment perspective, investors can make more informed decisions and navigate the cryptocurrency market effectively.

How to manage risk and make informed decisions

Investing in Bitcoin, the pioneering cryptocurrency, offers the potential for significant returns, diversification, and exposure to a rapidly evolving digital asset class. However, Bitcoin carries inherent risks like any investment due to its price volatility, regulatory uncertainty, and technological challenges. Investors must adopt a disciplined and risk-aware approach to navigate the cryptocurrency market effectively and make informed decisions.

Thorough research is the foundation of successful Bitcoin investing. Before entering the market, investors should dedicate time to understanding the fundamental principles of Bitcoin, its underlying technology, and the factors influencing its price movements. This research should include studying Bitcoin's whitepaper, analyzing the cryptocurrency's historical price trends, and staying informed about news and developments in the cryptocurrency space. A well-informed investor is better equipped to recognize potential risks and opportunities, making research a critical step in decision-making.

Setting clear investment goals and defining risk tolerance is essential to tailor a suitable investment strategy. Investors should establish specific objectives, such as long-term wealth accumulation, portfolio diversification, or short-term trading profits. Additionally, understanding and accepting individual risk tolerance is crucial in managing emotions during periods of market volatility. Determining the level of risk one is comfortable with helps avoid impulsive decisions driven by fear or greed.

Spreading assets over several asset classes, or diversification, is a basic risk management technique that lessens the impact of any one investment's performance on the portfolio as a whole. While Bitcoin can offer diversification benefits, it should not be the sole component of an investment portfolio. Investors should consider incorporating traditional assets like stocks, bonds, and real estate to balance risk and return potential.

Dollar-cost averaging is an investment technique that entails investing a specified amount of funds at regular intervals, regardless of the asset's price. This strategy mitigates the impact of market volatility on investment decisions and can be particularly effective in managing risk in the cryptocurrency market, where price fluctuations are common. By averaging the cost of acquiring Bitcoin over time, investors can avoid making emotionally driven decisions based on short-term price movements.

Implementing risk management measures is essential to protect investments from potential losses. One popular tactic is to place stop-loss orders, which cause a sale to happen automatically when the price of Bitcoin hits a given threshold. Stop-loss orders help limit potential losses during significant price declines. Additionally, investors can allocate only a portion of their investment capital to Bitcoin, leaving the rest in more stable assets.

The cryptocurrency market is susceptible to speculation, leading to excessive price volatility and misleading information. Investors should be cautious of rumors, hype, and unsubstantiated claims that can influence market sentiment. Relying on objective analysis and verified information is crucial to making well-informed decisions and avoiding impulsive actions based on market speculation.

Regulatory developments can have a major impact on the cryptocurrency market. Changes in regulations or government policies can influence investor sentiment and potentially affect Bitcoin's price. Investors should stay informed about regulatory developments in their respective jurisdictions and globally to anticipate potential changes in the cryptocurrency landscape.

Emotions can be significant in investment decisions, leading to fear-driven selling during market downturns or FOMO-induced buying at the peak of a rally. Investors must remain rational and disciplined, adhering to their predetermined investment strategies and risk management techniques. Avoiding emotional trading is key to making well-calculated decisions in the cryptocurrency market.

The cryptocurrency market is not resistant to scams and fraudulent schemes. Unsolicited investment offers, returns that are guaranteed, and ventures with little information or transparency should all raise red flags for investors. Conducting due diligence on investment opportunities and avoiding suspicious schemes is crucial in protecting one's capital from potential scams.

For investors who are new to Bitcoin or uncertain about their investment decisions, seeking professional advice can be beneficial. Financial advisors and investment professionals with expertise in cryptocurrency can provide insights and guidance tailored to an individual's financial situation and investment goals.

In conclusion, Bitcoin investing offers potential opportunities for growth and diversification, but it also carries inherent risks that must be managed prudently. Conducting thorough research, setting clear investment goals, diversifying the investment portfolio, and implementing risk management measures are essential strategies for managing risk in the cryptocurrency market. Staying informed about regulatory developments, being cautious of market speculation, and keeping emotions in check contributes to making well-informed decisions. As with any investment, seeking professional advice and adhering to a disciplined approach are key to effectively navigating the dynamic and evolving world of Bitcoin investing. By adopting these strategies and principles, investors can enhance their chances of success and mitigate potential risks in the cryptocurrency market.

CHAPTER V

Developing a Solid Bitcoin Investment Strategy

Setting clear investment goals

Investing in Bitcoin, the pioneering cryptocurrency, has become increasingly popular as more individuals and institutions seek exposure to the digital asset market. However, before diving into the world of Bitcoin investing, it is essential to establish clear investment goals. Setting well-defined objectives provides a roadmap for the investment journey and helps manage risk and aligns investment decisions with personal financial aspirations.

The first step in setting clear investment goals is understanding why one invests in Bitcoin. Investors should ask themselves what they hope to achieve through their investments. Some common investment goals in Bitcoin investing include capital appreciation, portfolio diversification, wealth preservation, and hedging against inflation or economic uncertainties. By understanding individual investment goals, investors can tailor their strategies and risk tolerance accordingly.

Investing in Bitcoin carries inherent risks, primarily due to the cryptocurrency's price volatility and the dynamic nature of the market. Defining risk tolerance involves understanding how much volatility an investor can endure without being emotionally affected. Different individuals have different risk tolerances, which can influence the allocation of funds to Bitcoin in the overall investment portfolio. Investors with higher risk tolerance may

allocate a more significant portion of their funds to Bitcoin, while those with lower risk tolerance may take a more conservative approach.

The investment horizon refers to the duration for which an investor plans to hold their Bitcoin investments. It can range from short-term, where investors seek to profit from price fluctuations, to long-term, where investors aim to hold Bitcoin for an extended period, anticipating its value to appreciate significantly. Identifying the investment horizon helps determine the appropriate investment strategy, risk management techniques, and the level of commitment required.

Given the asset's historical price volatility, setting realistic expectations is crucial in Bitcoin investing. While Bitcoin has shown impressive price appreciation over the years, investors should avoid setting overly ambitious or unrealistic return expectations. Instead, investors should base their projections on historical performance, market trends, and the underlying fundamentals of Bitcoin.

By distributing investments over several assets, diversification serves as a risk management tactic that lessens exposure to the performance of any single investment. While Bitcoin can offer diversification benefits, investors should consider how much of their overall portfolio they want to allocate to cryptocurrencies, including Bitcoin. Diversifying across different asset classes can help mitigate the risks associated with Bitcoin's price volatility.

Investors must evaluate their personal financial situation, including income, expenses, debts, and existing investments, before committing funds to Bitcoin. Understanding one's financial capacity to invest in Bitcoin ensures that the investment does not compromise essential financial needs or lead to financial stress.

Bitcoin investments may have tax implications depending on the jurisdiction and the nature of the investment. Investors should be aware of the tax regulations related to cryptocurrency investing in their country and consider the potential impact on their overall investment returns.

Having a clear exit strategy is essential in Bitcoin investing, particularly for short-term traders or those with specific financial goals. An exit strategy outlines the conditions under which investors plan to sell their Bitcoin holdings. This can be based on achieving a particular price target, reaching a certain profit level, or in response to changing market conditions. A well-defined exit strategy helps prevent emotional decision-making and meets investment goals.

Regularly reviewing and reassessing investment goals allows investors to stay on track and make necessary adjustments to their investment strategies. Investors should be flexible and open to adjusting their goals based on changing market conditions and personal financial situations.

For investors who are new to Bitcoin or uncertain about setting clear investment goals, seeking professional advice can be beneficial. Financial advisors and investment professionals with expertise in cryptocurrency investing can provide valuable insights and guidance tailored to individual financial circumstances and goals.

In conclusion, setting clear investment goals is a critical step in Bitcoin investing. Understanding investment objectives, defining risk tolerance, identifying the investment horizon, setting realistic expectations, considering diversification, evaluating personal financial situations, assessing tax implications, having a clear exit strategy, and regularly reviewing and reassessing goals are essential to setting clear investment goals in Bitcoin investing. By establishing well-defined objectives and aligning investment decisions with personal aspirations, investors can enhance their chances of success and effectively navigate the dynamic and evolving world of Bitcoin investing. Seeking professional advice can provide additional support and expertise to optimize investment strategies and achieve long-term financial objectives.

Choosing the right investment approach (long-term vs. short-term)

The innovative cryptocurrency Bitcoin has drawn interest from institutional and individual investors worldwide. Investors must make a critical decision as the digital asset market develops: deciding which investing strategy best suits their risk tolerance and financial objectives. There are two primary investment approaches in Bitcoin investing - long-term and short-term.

Long-term Bitcoin investing involves purchasing and holding the digital asset with the expectation that its value will appreciate over an extended period. Long-term investors have a "buy and hold" mentality, seeking to benefit from Bitcoin's potential to serve as a store of value and a hedge against traditional financial market risks. This approach needs patience and a willingness to weather short-term price fluctuations in exchange for potential significant returns over the long run.

One of the main advantages of long-term Bitcoin investing is that it enable investors to avoid the stress and complexities of frequent trading. Instead of trying to time the market, long-term investors focus on the underlying fundamentals of Bitcoin, such as its limited supply, utility, and growing adoption. Long-term investing also reduces transaction costs and tax liabilities associated with frequent trading. However, long-term Bitcoin investing has its challenges. The digital asset market can be highly volatile, and investors must be prepared to endure significant price fluctuations during their holding period.

Moreover, long-term investing requires a deep understanding of Bitcoin's technology and potential global economic applications.

Short-term Bitcoin investing, also known as trading or active investing, involves buying and selling Bitcoin within a relatively short period to capitalize on price movements. Short-term traders utilize technical analysis, market indicators, and chart patterns to identify short-term trends and make quick investment decisions. This approach can appeal to those seeking to profit from short-term price swings and potentially generate quick returns.

One of the advantages of short-term Bitcoin investing is the potential for higher liquidity and more frequent trading opportunities. Short-term traders can take advantage of upward and downward price movements, potentially profiting in bullish and bearish market conditions. Additionally, short-term trading provides a more dynamic and engaging experience for investors who enjoy actively managing their portfolios. However, short-term Bitcoin investing comes with its own set of challenges and risks. Short-term traders must be highly disciplined and deeply understand technical analysis. The cryptocurrency market is known for its volatility, and short-term traders must be prepared to manage risks actively. Frequent trading can also increase transaction costs and tax implications, potentially eating into profits.

Several factors should be considered when deciding between a long-term or short-term investment approach in Bitcoin investing. Risk tolerance is one such factor, as long-term investing is generally considered less risky due to its focus on the asset's long-term potential. In contrast, short-term trading requires a higher risk tolerance due to the rapid price fluctuations and the need for quick decision-making. Additionally, investors should consider their time horizon when choosing an investment approach. Long-term investing requires a longer commitment, while short-term trading may be more suitable for those with a more active and shorter time horizon.

Market knowledge and experience are essential considerations. Short-term trading requires a more in-depth understanding of technical analysis and market dynamics, so investors should assess their level of knowledge and experience before engaging in active trading. Financial goals are another critical factor in choosing the right investment approach. Long-term investing may be more suitable for those seeking capital appreciation and wealth accumulation over time. In contrast, short-term trading may appeal to those looking for quick profits and short-term gains. Additionally, investors should consider the impact of transaction costs and taxes on their overall returns. Frequent trading may have an impact on net gains because it may increase transaction costs and tax obligations.

Investors may sometimes combine long-term and short-term approaches in their Bitcoin investment strategy. This approach, known as a hybrid or balanced strategy, involves holding a core position in Bitcoin for the long term while engaging in short-term trading to take advantage of price fluctuations. The balanced strategy allows investors to benefit from both the potential long-term appreciation of Bitcoin and short-term trading opportunities.

Regardless of the chosen investment approach, diversification remains a fundamental risk management strategy in Bitcoin investing. Diversifying across different assets, including cryptocurrencies and traditional investments, can help mitigate risk and provide a more balanced portfolio. For investors unsure about which investment approach is best suited to their financial goals and risk tolerance, seeking professional advice can be beneficial. Financial advisors and investment professionals with expertise in cryptocurrency investing can provide valuable insights and guidance tailored to individual circumstances.

In conclusion, choosing the right investment approach in Bitcoin investing is a critical decision that should be based on individual financial goals, risk tolerance, time horizon, and market knowledge. Long-term investing offers potential for capital appreciation and the benefits of a "buy and hold" strategy, while short-term trading presents opportunities for quick profits and active portfolio management. Investors may also consider a hybrid approach to combine the advantages of both strategies. Diversification and seeking professional advice are key components of a well-rounded Bitcoin investment strategy. Ultimately, a thoughtful and informed decision will help investors successfully navigate the dynamic and evolving world of Bitcoin investing.

Diversification and portfolio management in the cryptocurrency market

The cryptocurrency market has emerged as a disruptive and highly dynamic asset class, attracting both retail and institutional investors seeking opportunities for high returns. However, the extreme volatility and inherent risks associated with cryptocurrencies make portfolio management and risk mitigation crucial for investors. Diversification is a fundamental strategy employed to spread risk across different assets within a portfolio.

Diversification is an investment strategy that spreads investments across different assets and asset classes to reduce exposure to any single investment's performance. By diversifying, investors aim to achieve a more balanced risk-return profile and enhance the stability of their overall portfolio. In the cryptocurrency market, diversification is essential due to the highly volatile nature of individual digital assets. Cryptocurrencies can experience rapid price swings, and the performance of any single cryptocurrency can be influenced by a myriad of factors, including market sentiment, regulatory developments, technological advancements, and macroeconomic conditions.

Diversification in the cryptocurrency market offers several benefits to investors. Firstly, it mitigates risk by spreading investments across various cryptocurrencies. This reduces their exposure to the idiosyncratic risks associated with individual assets, as a decline in the value of one cryptocurrency may be offset by the performance of others in the portfolio, limiting potential losses. Secondly, diversification can lead to a more stable portfolio since different cryptocurrencies may respond differently to market events, reducing overall portfolio volatility. Thirdly, a well-diversified portfolio may have the potential for higher returns. While cryptocurrencies are known for their high volatility, some assets may outperform others during specific market conditions. A diversified portfolio increases the likelihood of participating in the growth of top-performing cryptocurrencies. Finally, diversification provides exposure to multiple use cases. Cryptocurrencies serve various use cases, ranging from a store of value to platforms for decentralized applications. Diversification allows investors to gain exposure to different projects and their underlying technologies.

Despite the benefits, diversifying a cryptocurrency portfolio comes with its own set of challenges. One major challenge is the limited correlation in the cryptocurrency market. Cryptocurrencies have shown limited correlation with traditional financial markets and even among cryptocurrencies themselves. Identifying assets that move independently during market fluctuations can be challenging. Additionally, diversification demands significant research intensity. With many cryptocurrencies available, conducting thorough research to assess each asset's fundamentals, technology, and long-term viability requires significant effort. The market immaturity of some projects adds complexity to the process, as some projects may lack proven track records or adequate liquidity, making it challenging to assess their potential accurately. Moreover, managing a diverse cryptocurrency portfolio demands secure storage and risk management practices to safeguard digital assets from theft or hacks.

To effectively diversify a cryptocurrency portfolio, investors should consider several best practices. Firstly, risk assessment is crucial. Evaluating risk tolerance and investment goals before building a portfolio will help determine the appropriate asset allocation. Riskier investments may warrant a smaller allocation within the portfolio. Secondly, asset allocation plays a significant role. Investors should allocate funds across different cryptocurrencies, considering factors such as market capitalization, liquidity, technology, team, and growth potential. Thirdly, considering asset types is essential. Diversification should be limited to different cryptocurrencies and across different types of assets, such as digital currencies, utility tokens, and security tokens. Regularly reviewing and rebalancing the portfolio to maintain the desired asset allocation is crucial. Market dynamics and performance may lead to imbalances over time, and periodic rebalancing helps ensure the portfolio remains aligned with the investor's goals and risk profile. It is also important to avoid overexposure to any single cryptocurrency. Allocating an excessive portion of the portfolio to a single asset can increase the risk associated with that particular asset's performance. Implementing robust risk management strategies, such as stop-loss orders and position sizing, will help limit potential losses during market downturns.

When considering portfolio management, investors can choose between active and passive approaches. Active management involves making frequent adjustments to the portfolio based on market trends and investment opportunities. Active managers seek to outperform the market and take advantage of short-term price movements. On the other hand, passive management involves maintaining a fixed allocation to cryptocurrencies and rebalancing the portfolio periodically. The long-term goal of passive strategies is to generate market returns by tracking benchmarks in the market. Investors who want a more hands-off approach to managing their portfolios tend to choose passive management, whilst those who are ready to take on greater risks in the hopes of potentially larger returns may favor active management.

In addition to the internal factors involved in portfolio management, external factors can also influence the diversification and management of a cryptocurrency portfolio. Market sentiment, regulatory developments, technological advancements, and macroeconomic conditions can impact the performance of cryptocurrencies. Staying knowledgeable about these factors and their potential effects on the market is essential for prudent portfolio management.

For investors unsure about building and managing a diversified cryptocurrency portfolio, seeking professional advice can be beneficial. Financial advisors and investment professionals with expertise in the cryptocurrency market can provide valuable insights and guidance tailored to individual financial goals and risk profiles.

In conclusion, diversification and portfolio management are essential strategies for navigating the dynamic and highly volatile cryptocurrency market. A well-diversified portfolio can help investors mitigate risks, enhance stability, and potentially achieve higher returns. While challenges exist, careful research, risk assessment, and adherence to best practices can assist in building a successful cryptocurrency portfolio. Investors must take into account their risk tolerance, investment goals, and their time horizon when making investment decisions, and may choose between active and passive portfolio management approaches. As the cryptocurrency market evolves, staying informed and seeking professional advice will remain crucial elements of successful portfolio management in this emerging asset class.

CHAPTER VI

Technical Analysis for Bitcoin Trading

Introduction to technical analysis and its relevance in cryptocurrency trading

A vibrant and profitable industry, cryptocurrency trading has drawn investors looking to profit on the possibility of large profits in a volatile market. In this fast-paced environment, where prices can experience dramatic fluctuations within short timeframes, traders rely on various strategies to make informed decisions. One prominent approach that has gained widespread traction is technical analysis. Technical analysis involves studying historical market data, primarily price and trading volume, to forecast future price movements and identify potential trading opportunities. This section will delve into the foundational concepts of technical analysis, explore its key principles, the tools and indicators used, highlight its relevance within the cryptocurrency trading landscape, discuss its limitations, and emphasize the significance of continuous learning and seeking professional guidance.

Fundamentally, technical analysis is predicated on the idea that historical price fluctuations might reveal information about upcoming price trends. This methodology operates under the assumption that market participants' behavior repeats itself due to consistent human responses to market conditions. Unlike fundamental analysis, which delves into a cryptocurrency's intrinsic value by considering factors such as company financials and macroeconomic indicators, technical analysis focuses solely on analyzing price action and historical patterns to make trading decisions.

Several key principles form the foundation of technical analysis:

The idea that a cryptocurrency's price chart already represents all pertinent information that could influence its price is one of the core tenets of technical analysis. This principle implies that market fundamentals, news, and events are all assimilated into the price, rendering it the most accurate representation of market sentiment and expectations.

A cornerstone of technical analysis is the concept that prices move in trends. Cryptocurrencies exhibit trends that can be bullish (rising), bearish (falling), or sideways (consolidating). Recognizing and following these trends is critical to making informed trading decisions and capitalizing on market movements.

The past tends to repeat itself, and technical analysts leverage historical price patterns to anticipate potential future price movements. Recognizable patterns, such as support and resistance levels, chart formations, and trendlines, help traders predict where prices might be headed.

Technical analysis assumes that market participants' emotions and psychology significantly influence price movements. Patterns and signals on price charts are often interpreted as manifestations of market psychology, reflecting sentiments such as fear, greed, and uncertainty.

Technical analysis employs various tools and indicators to assist traders in interpreting price charts and identifying trends. These tools include but are not limited to moving averages, support and resistance levels, trendlines, and chart patterns including head and shoulders, double tops, and triangles. Additionally, technical analysts rely on indicators like Relative Strength Index (or RSI), Moving Average Convergence Divergence (or MACD), and Bollinger Bands to glean insights into market conditions and potential turning points.

Technical analysis holds significant relevance within the cryptocurrency trading sphere for several compelling reasons:

Cryptocurrency markets are renowned for their extreme volatility, making them fertile ground for technical analysis. Prices can experience substantial fluctuations over short periods, offering traders abundant opportunities for profitable trades.

Unlike traditional financial markets where established fundamentals guide valuation, cryptocurrencies often lack universally accepted fundamentals. Traditional valuation metrics may not apply effectively, rendering technical analysis a more pragmatic approach to assess price movements.

Many cryptocurrency traders engage in short-term trading to profit from rapid price movements within intraday or short-term timeframes. Technical analysis provides tools and insights that enable traders to make quick decisions and capitalize on these fleeting opportunities.

Market sentiment, news, and social media trends can profoundly influence cryptocurrency prices. Technical analysis serves as a crucial tool for gauging market sentiment through the interpretation of price patterns and indicators.

While technical analysis offers valuable insights, it is essential to acknowledge its limitations and criticisms. Detractors argue that technical analysis can be subjective, with interpretations of patterns and signals potentially varying among analysts. Moreover, technical analysis may not fully account for sudden and market-changing events, such as regulatory announcements or technological vulnerabilities, which can defy historical patterns and override technical signals.

Many traders combine technical analysis with other methodologies, such as fundamental analysis and sentiment analysis, to obtain a more comprehensive view of the market. By incorporating multiple approaches, traders aim to mitigate risks associated with depending solely on one method and to capitalize on a broader spectrum of insights.

Technical analysis is not a static skill but an evolving one that necessitates continuous learning and practice. The cryptocurrency market is dynamic, and new patterns, indicators, and trends emerge over time. Traders must remain up-to-date with the latest developments in technical analysis to remain effective in their strategies.

For novice traders or those seeking to enhance their technical analysis skills, seeking guidance from experienced traders or professional advisors is highly beneficial. These experts can provide insights into effective strategies, the interpretation of various indicators, and the application of technical analysis in real-world trading scenarios.

Technical analysis plays a pivotal role in the toolkit of cryptocurrency traders, providing a systematic approach to deciphering historical price patterns, identifying trends, and gauging market sentiment. By grasping its core principles, mastering various tools and indicators, and recognizing its applicability in the volatile cryptocurrency market, traders can make more informed decisions and navigate the intricacies of digital asset trading. However, it is crucial to acknowledge technical analysis's limitations and consider it a component within a broader trading strategy. As the cryptocurrency landscape evolves and matures, adapting and honing technical analysis skills will remain essential for successful trading in this rapidly changing and highly competitive environment.

Key technical indicators and how to interpret them

Technical analysis is an indispensable tool in the trading world, and its significance is particularly pronounced in the volatile and ever-evolving realm of cryptocurrencies. Traders employ various methods to decipher price movements and forecast potential market trends. Among these methods, technical indicators are crucial components that offer valuable insights by quantifying and visually representing market data. This section explores the foundational concepts of technical indicators, delves into several key indicators commonly used in cryptocurrency trading, and discusses how to interpret them effectively to make well-informed trading decisions.

Technical indicators are mathematical calculations derived from historical data such as price, volume, or open interest. These calculations result in graphical representations that help traders identify patterns, trends, and potential reversal points. In essence, technical indicators bridge the gap between raw market data and actionable insights, enabling traders to make more informed and educated decisions in their trading endeavors.

Moving averages stand as one of the fundamental and widely employed technical indicators. They smoothen price data by creating a continuously updated average price over a specified period. Two primary types of moving averages exist: the Simple Moving Average (or SMA) and the Exponential Moving Average (or FMA). The SMA offers a straightforward average of prices, whereas the EMA places greater emphasis on recent prices, making it more responsive to recent price changes. The interpretation of moving averages involves observing crossovers between different moving averages. Specifically, a shorter-term moving average crossing above a longer-term moving average could signal an emerging uptrend, while the reverse scenario may indicate a potential downtrend.

Another crucial technical indicator is the Relative Strength Index (RSI), which operates as a momentum oscillator. The RSI offers insights into potential overbought and oversold conditions by measuring the speed and change of price movements. With a range from 0 to 100, values exceeding 70 suggest overbought conditions, while values falling below 30 indicate oversold conditions. Traders often use the RSI to identify potential reversal points and gauge the strength of an existing trend. For instance, an RSI above 70 may imply an impending pullback, whereas an RSI below 30 might signify a forthcoming price bounce.

Moving Average Convergence Divergence (MACD) represents another versatile technical indicator that integrates moving averages to provide insights into momentum and trend direction. Consisting of a MACD line and a signal line, the MACD generates signals through crossovers and divergence patterns. Specifically, a MACD line crossing above the signal line may indicate a potential bullish trend, while a crossover below might signal a possible bearish trend. The divergence between the MACD and price can offer a valuable signal for potential trend reversals.

Bollinger Bands constitute yet another prominent technical indicator. These bands consist of a central band, typically an SMA or EMA, flanked by an upper and lower band. The upper and lower bands illustrate standard deviations from the central band. Bollinger Bands dynamically expand and contract in response to market volatility. These bands assist traders in identifying potential overbought and oversold conditions and periods characterized by heightened volatility. For instance, when prices touch the upper band, it might indicate an overbought condition and an impending pullback. Conversely, a touch of the lower band may signal an oversold condition and a potential price bounce.

The Stochastic Oscillator is yet another tool in the arsenal of technical indicators. This oscillator compares the closing price of a cryptocurrency to its price range over a specified period. It offers insights similar to the RSI regarding overbought and oversold conditions. However, the Stochastic Oscillator emphasizes the relationship between the closing price and the price range, rather than focusing solely on price momentum. The interpretation of the Stochastic Oscillator involves observing crossovers, identifying overbought and oversold zones, and recognizing divergence patterns.

Interpreting technical indicators effectively requires understanding their mathematical underpinnings and recognizing their relevance in specific market conditions. While technical indicators undoubtedly provide invaluable insights, they are most potent when used with other market data. Traders often combine multiple indicators and analyze them in tandem with price patterns, volume, and other pertinent market metrics. Several considerations are essential when interpreting technical indicators.

First and foremost, the importance of confirmatory signals cannot be overstated. Relying on multiple indicators that yield confirming signals can significantly enhance the reliability of predictions. Seeking confluence across different indicators adds a layer of validation to the trading decision-making process. Moreover, market context plays a pivotal role in interpreting technical indicators accurately. Different indicators may yield varying results based on the prevailing market conditions, such as trending, ranging, or high volatility periods. Additionally, the timeframe used for analysis holds significant implications. Indicators can behave differently when applied to varying timeframes. Short-term traders might employ indicators on shorter timeframes for intraday decisions, whereas long-term investors might focus on longer timeframes to capture broader trends. Selecting a timeframe that aligns with the trader's strategy and objectives is crucial.

Traders must also exercise caution regarding the occurrence of false signals. Just as technical indicators can provide valuable insights, they can also generate false or misleading signals. Risk management strategies are imperative to mitigate potential losses stemming from erroneous predictions. Backtesting, or historical analysis using indicators, can provide insights into how indicators have performed in the past. While past performance does not guarantee future results, backtesting enables traders to understand how indicators behaved under different market conditions, thereby refining their interpretations.

Furthermore, the learning curve associated with effectively interpreting technical indicators should not be underestimated. Mastery of each indicator's nuances demands practice, experimentation, and continuous learning. Gaining familiarity with the behavior of indicators in various market scenarios enhances a trader's ability to leverage them accurately.

In conclusion, technical indicators serve as essential tools in the toolkit of traders navigating the complexities of the cryptocurrency market. Traders gain insights into price trends, momentum shifts, and potential reversal points by grasping the principles underlying key indicators like moving averages, RSI, MACD, Bollinger Bands, and the Stochastic Oscillator. Nevertheless, effective interpretation necessitates a holistic approach considering multiple indicators, market context, timeframes, and confirmatory signals. Just as technical analysis itself is a skill that requires ongoing practice and learning, mastering the art of interpreting technical indicators is a journey that sharpens traders' capacity to make sound and potentially profitable trading decisions in the ever-changing realm of cryptocurrency trading.

Analyzing price charts and identifying trends

Price charts visually represent the ebb and flow of market movements, encapsulating the intricate dance of supply and demand within financial landscapes. In the context of the ever-fluctuating and dynamic cryptocurrency trading realm, the skill of analyzing price charts and identifying trends stands as a cornerstone for traders navigating this complex terrain. This section explores the art of price chart analysis, delving into the various manifestations of trends, elucidating the significance of chart patterns, and illuminating the paramount importance of contextual understanding to make well-informed trading decisions.

Central to this understanding is the grasp of price charts as a historical record. These charts depict the historical journey of an asset's price over time. In cryptocurrency trading, they serve as the visual backbone, portraying the value of a specific cryptocurrency on the vertical axis juxtaposed with time on the horizontal axis. Each data point on the chart signifies a unique price at a particular point in time, collectively forming an unbroken line that visually encapsulates the asset's price trajectory. Different chart types, like line charts, bar charts, and candlestick charts, offer distinct lenses through which traders perceive price movements, each holding its own insights.

Similar to the currents in a flowing river, trends hold the key to deciphering the market's underlying dynamics. Trends, as patterns of sustained movement in a specific direction, unveil a fundamental layer of the market's behavior. Among the archetypes of trends, three primary manifestations emerge:

First, the "uptrend" – a manifestation of bullish sentiment. This phenomenon surfaces when prices consistently mark higher highs and higher lows. This sequence indicates robust buying momentum and reflects an environment of positive market sentiment. In such conditions, traders are inclined to seize the opportunities to enter the market, anticipating further appreciation of prices.

Second, the "downtrend" – a portrayal of bearish sentiment. This trend materializes when prices consistently create lower highs and lower lows. Such a pattern showcases sustained selling pressure and a prevailing negative sentiment. In the presence of a downtrend, traders often contemplate actions like short-selling or prudently avoiding long positions to evade potential losses.

Finally, the "sideways trend" – a realm of market indecision. This pattern unfolds when prices oscillate within a relatively confined range without a consistent upward or downward trajectory. Such trends may suggest a phase of uncertainty, prompting traders to exercise caution in their strategies.

As traders immerse themselves in the realm of chart analysis, an arsenal of chart patterns emerges, offering insights into potential future price movements. These patterns often serve as harbingers of anticipated market behavior. Chart patterns can be broadly classified into two categories: continuation patterns and reversal patterns.

Continuation patterns, the first class, signify that an ongoing trend will likely sustain its course following the pattern's resolution. Examples include the likes of flags, pennants, and triangles – each offering traders a glimpse into potential entry or augmentation points within an existing trend.

Conversely, the second category – reversal patterns – signifies that the current trend might be nearing an inflection point. Patterns like the head and shoulders, double tops, and double bottoms capture traders' attention by signifying potential trend reversals. These patterns function as critical tools in the trader's toolkit, allowing them to anticipate shifts in the market sentiment and adapt their positions accordingly.

However, the mastery of analyzing price charts transcends mere pattern recognition. It necessitates an integration of the broader context that envelops the market's movements. Contextual analysis, which considers factors such as market sentiment, news events, macroeconomic developments, and even social media trends, imbues the analysis with a holistic perspective. For instance, the sudden emergence of a pivotal news announcement can swiftly lead to a trend reversal or an abrupt price breakout, illustrating the vital role that contextual awareness plays in understanding the market's intricate tapestry.

In this pursuit of deciphering the mysteries within price charts, traders wield many tools to enhance their understanding. Among these tools are the venerable support and resistance levels. Support levels denote price points where a cryptocurrency has historically found buying interest, effectively arresting further price declines. Conversely, resistance levels denote the junctures where selling pressure historically emerges, capping the upward movement of prices. Identifying these levels serves as a compass for traders, helping them anticipate potential market momentum shifts.

Trendlines, too, stand as instrumental aides in this voyage of analysis. These diagonal lines, etched onto the chart, link successive higher lows in an uptrend or lower highs in a downtrend. Trendlines offer traders insight into the trajectory and strength of a prevailing trend, potentially serving as levels of support or resistance in the market.

Moving averages, another tool in the trader's repertoire, emerge as a visual representation of the underlying trend smoothed over a specified period. Traders harness moving averages to unveil the trend's overarching direction and pinpoint potential entry or exit points in their strategies.

Furthermore, the analysis of price charts is augmented by exploring volume patterns. Volume, synonymous with the number of assets traded, follows the footsteps of price movements. Its analysis in conjunction with price fluctuations can validate trends and patterns, adding a layer of confirmation. For instance, a breakout accompanied by high trading volume may signify the robustness of a newly emerging trend.

Interpreting these intricate price patterns mandates the harmonious interplay of technical analysis acumen and market intuition. It is a multidimensional endeavor that embraces a medley of tools and indicators to validate and refine findings. Moreover, a diverse timescale perspective offers a multifaceted view of the market's oscillations, enabling traders to capture both immediate and long-term trends, thereby augmenting their grasp of the market's dynamics.

Analyzing price charts and identifying trends is a voyage that combines art and science in cryptocurrency trading. Those who master this art acquire an enhanced lens to observe the market's heartbeat, allowing for more calculated and informed trading decisions. Proficiency in identifying various trend manifestations, understanding the significance of chart patterns, employing contextual understanding, and effectively utilizing an array of tools equips traders to navigate the unpredictable cryptocurrency landscape with enhanced poise.

Furthermore, this skill empowers traders to capitalize on opportunities while adroitly managing risks. As the cryptocurrency landscape continues to evolve, the skill of analyzing price charts and identifying trends remains a lodestar guiding traders through the labyrinthine corridors of this dynamic, ever-transforming market.

CHAPTER VII

Fundamental Analysis for Bitcoin Investing

Understanding fundamental analysis and its role in evaluating cryptocurrencies

In the intricate world of cryptocurrency investing, understanding the underlying value of digital assets is paramount. This section embarks on a journey to unravel the concept of fundamental analysis and its pivotal role in assessing the worth of cryptocurrencies. By delving into the methodologies of evaluating project fundamentals, exploring key factors that influence cryptocurrency value, and deciphering the challenges inherent in this approach, investors can navigate the complexities of the cryptocurrency market with greater insight and strategic foresight.

Fundamental analysis, often associated with traditional financial markets, is a framework that assesses the intrinsic value of an asset. Fundamental analysis offers a grounded approach in the cryptocurrency realm, where volatility reigns and speculation abounds. This methodology involves evaluating the project's underlying technology, team, market potential, use cases, and broader ecosystem to ascertain its long-term viability and potential for growth. While it requires a deep understanding of both technology and market dynamics, fundamental analysis seeks to identify cryptocurrencies with solid foundations amid the noise and hype.

The cornerstone of fundamental analysis is a meticulous evaluation of project fundamentals. This encompasses various aspects, including the technology powering the cryptocurrency, the team behind its development, the use cases it addresses, and the strength of its partnerships. Scrutinizing the technical whitepaper and codebase allows investors to assess the innovation and practicality of the project's solutions. The development team's competence and experience indicate their ability to execute the project's vision. Evaluating the broader ecosystem and community engagement provides insights into adoption potential and overall market sentiment.

Understanding a cryptocurrency's potential for adoption and utility is pivotal in fundamental analysis. While technological innovation lays the foundation, real-world use cases drive demand and value. Cryptocurrencies that offer solutions to real-world problems or streamline existing processes are more likely to garner adoption. Additionally, analyzing the extent of partnerships, collaborations, and integrations within the industry provides a glimpse into the cryptocurrency's ability to penetrate existing markets and catalyze change.

Cryptocurrency markets are not isolated entities but interconnected with the broader global economy. Factors such as macroeconomic trends, geopolitical events, and regulatory developments impact the cryptocurrency market's dynamics. For instance, regulatory clarity or uncertainty can significantly influence investor sentiment. Understanding how these macroeconomic factors intertwine with the cryptocurrency landscape allows investors to make more informed predictions and adjust their strategies accordingly.

Tokenomics, the study of a cryptocurrency's supply and distribution mechanisms, is an integral component of fundamental analysis. Scarcity plays a pivotal role in determining value. Cryptocurrencies with limited supplies, such as Bitcoin's capped supply of 21 million coins, are often associated with potential for value appreciation over time. Understanding token distribution, inflation rates, and mechanisms for rewards and governance provides insights into the alignment of incentives among stakeholders.

While fundamental analysis offers a robust framework, it comes with its own set of challenges and limitations. Cryptocurrency projects operate in a rapidly evolving landscape, and information can quickly become outdated. Additionally, assessing the qualitative aspects of projects, such as team competence and market potential, can be subjective and prone to biases. The lack of standardized metrics and transparency in cryptocurrency further complicates the evaluation process.

While fundamental analysis focuses on the underlying value of a cryptocurrency, it is essential to recognize that a myriad of factors influences the market's behavior. Balancing fundamental analysis with technical analysis, which examines price trends and patterns, offers a more holistic view. A cryptocurrency with strong fundamentals may still experience price volatility due to external market forces. Therefore, a comprehensive approach integrating both methodologies empowers investors to make well-informed decisions.

In conclusion, fundamental analysis is a compass in the labyrinthine cryptocurrency landscape. Investors can unearth hidden gems amidst the noise and speculation by evaluating project fundamentals, market potential, macroeconomic factors, tokenomics, and supply dynamics. While challenges exist, such as outdated information and subjectivity, a careful assessment of cryptocurrencies through a fundamental lens provides a grounded approach to investing. Ultimately, a combination of fundamental and technical analysis equips investors with the tools to navigate the complexities of the cryptocurrency market and make decisions driven by a deeper understanding of value, potential, and market dynamics. As the cryptocurrency ecosystem evolves, the role of fundamental analysis remains a beacon for discerning investors seeking to uncover genuine value and seize opportunities in this ever-evolving digital frontier.

Factors that influence Bitcoin's value and price movements

The value and price movements of Bitcoin, the pioneering cryptocurrency, are subjects of intense fascination and speculation in the financial world. Bitcoin's decentralized nature and limited supply contribute to its unique market dynamics, where various internal and external factors intersect to shape its value and drive price fluctuations. This section delves into the multifaceted realm of Bitcoin's value determinants and the intricate web of influences that propel its price movements. From macroeconomic factors to regulatory developments and market sentiment, this exploration aims to shed light on the complex tapestry that governs Bitcoin's price discovery.

At the core of Bitcoin's value proposition lies its finite supply. Bitcoin is fundamentally different from typical fiat currencies because of its scarcity, which is designed to be limited to a maximum number of 21 million coins, typical fiat currencies are subject to inflationary forces. This scarcity imbues Bitcoin with a store of value characteristic, similar to precious metals like gold. As demand for Bitcoin grows, its limited supply can increase its price pressure. Conversely, scarcity can amplify selling pressure in times of heightened market activity. Psychology plays a crucial role in Bitcoin's price movements. Positive news, mainstream adoption, and endorsements by influential figures can elevate market sentiment, attracting new investors and triggering price rallies. Conversely, negative news, security breaches, or regulatory crackdowns can erode trust and trigger selloffs. The perception of Bitcoin as a speculative asset or a hedge against economic instability can sway sentiment and consequently impact price trends.

The regulatory landscape surrounding Bitcoin significantly influences its value and price movements. Regulatory clarity and acceptance can encourage mainstream adoption and investment. Conversely, stringent regulations or bans can shadow the cryptocurrency's future prospects, impacting demand and causing price volatility. The interplay between regulatory agencies, governments, and the evolving nature of the technology creates an environment where regulatory news can lead to dramatic price swings.

Bitcoin's underlying technology, the blockchain, is subject to continuous innovation. Technological developments, such as scalability solutions or transaction speed and cost improvements, can impact user experience and adoption rates. Positive advancements can attract more users and investors, driving demand and potentially boosting prices. Conversely, technological vulnerabilities or security concerns can lead to selloffs and negative sentiment.

The simplicity with which Bitcoin can be bought or sold without having a substantial impact on its price is a key factor in determining the value of Bitcoin. Higher liquidity fosters smoother price discovery and reduces the impact of large trades on the market. Trading volume, the total value of assets traded, also influences price trends. High trading volume can indicate strong market interest, while low volume may signify lackluster demand or potential price manipulation.

Bitcoin's value is intricately connected to broader economic trends. Economic instability, currency devaluation, and negative interest rates can lead to increased interest in Bitcoin as a store of value and hedge against traditional financial risks. Geopolitical tensions and macroeconomic events can trigger safe-haven flows into Bitcoin, influencing its price dynamics. Conversely, economic growth and stability periods may see reduced demand for alternative assets like Bitcoin.

The degree of Bitcoin's adoption and integration into various sectors of the economy also influences its value. Wider acceptance for payments, investment vehicles, and remittances can drive demand and increase its utility, subsequently impacting its value. Partnerships with traditional financial institutions, integrating Bitcoin into mainstream platforms, and creating financial products tied to Bitcoin can elevate its profile and boost demand.

The decentralized nature of the cryptocurrency market leaves it susceptible to manipulation, especially in its early stages. Large holders, often called "whales," can impact prices through substantial buy or sell orders. Coordinated efforts to inflate or deflate prices, known as "pump and dump" schemes, can distort price trends and erode market confidence.

Broader economic trends, such as inflation rates, interest rates, and economic growth can influence Bitcoin's value. Economic conditions that favor adopting alternative assets or safe-haven investments can drive demand for Bitcoin, impacting its price. Conversely, economic stability and growth periods may see reduced demand for alternative assets.

Media coverage and narratives surrounding Bitcoin can significantly impact its value and price movements. Positive coverage highlighting its potential applications or success stories can attract new investors and drive demand. Conversely, negative coverage or misconceptions about the technology can lead to selloffs and dampened sentiment.

In conclusion, Bitcoin's value and price movements are a confluence of technological, economic, regulatory, and psychological factors. Its scarcity, market sentiment, regulatory developments, technological innovations, liquidity, macroeconomic conditions, adoption trends, and even media influence interact in intricate ways to determine its value and drive price fluctuations. The evolving nature of the cryptocurrency landscape ensures that these influences remain dynamic and subject to change. Traders, investors, and enthusiasts alike navigate this landscape by observing and analyzing these factors, understanding their interplay, and adapting their strategies to capitalize on opportunities while managing risks in this fascinating and rapidly evolving market.

Analyzing news and events in the cryptocurrency space

The world of cryptocurrencies is a landscape characterized by rapid changes, technological innovations, and evolving regulations. In this dynamic environment, news and events are pivotal in shaping market sentiment, influencing price movements, and guiding investor decisions. This section delves into the critical art of analyzing news and events in the cryptocurrency space, exploring the types of news that impact the market, the methodologies for evaluating their significance, and the strategies traders and investors employ to navigate this information-rich landscape.

In the realm of cryptocurrencies, news and events can ignite rapid shifts in market sentiment and trigger substantial price movements. Positive news, such as regulatory endorsements, partnerships with established companies, technological advancements, or increased adoption, can foster a sense of optimism, attracting new investors and driving prices higher. Conversely, negative news, security breaches, regulatory crackdowns, or market manipulation incidents can erode trust, spark fear, and result in swift selloffs. Due to the high degree of volatility that characterizes the cryptocurrency market, it is very sensitive to a wide range of macroeconomic and micro-level events.

A wide array of news and events influences the cryptocurrency space. Regulatory developments are prominent, as decisions made by governments and regulatory bodies can significantly impact market sentiment. Technological advancements, such as protocol upgrades or new consensus mechanisms, can also wield considerable influence. Additionally, news related to security vulnerabilities, exchange hacks, and high-profile endorsements can have far-reaching consequences. Market-moving events might include initial coin offerings (ICOs), exchange token listings, and significant partnerships within the blockchain ecosystem.

Not all news and events carry equal weight in the cryptocurrency world. The ability to discern the significance of a particular piece of information is paramount. Traders and investors often employ a multifaceted approach to gauge the impact of news. Factors such as the source's credibility, the historical relevance of similar events, the potential implications for the technology or project, and the broader market sentiment are considered. News that aligns with the fundamental principles of decentralization, security, and adoption tends to hold more weight than speculative or sensationalized information.

Effective analysis of news and events requires a structured approach. Traders and investors often employ several strategies to stay informed and make informed decisions. Many utilize news aggregators and cryptocurrency-focused media outlets to track the latest developments. Social media platforms and online communities also play a role, providing real-time updates and discussions. Additionally, traders might employ sentiment analysis tools that utilize natural language processing to gauge a particular topic's prevailing sentiment. Combining these strategies enables individuals to comprehensively view the current landscape.

Not all news has an immediate impact on the market. Distinguishing between short-term and long-term influences is crucial. While certain news items can trigger rapid price fluctuations in the short term, their lasting impact may be limited. Conversely, developments that align with the long-term vision of a project or the overall industry can shape market trends over an extended period. An astute analysis accounts for both short-term volatility and the potential for enduring changes in the market landscape.

The cryptocurrency space is not immune to misinformation and rumors. Incorrect or misleading information has the potential to rapidly propagate and cause irrational price fluctuations in the market. A critical eye and a commitment to due diligence are imperative to counter this. Cross-referencing information from multiple credible sources and verifying claims before acting on them helps mitigate the risks associated with misinformation.

Effectively analyzing news and events in the cryptocurrency space necessitates a holistic perspective. Market-moving news rarely exists in isolation; it often interacts with broader trends, regulatory developments, and macroeconomic factors. Understanding these interconnected dynamics enables traders and investors to interpret news within the context of the larger market landscape, making more informed decisions.

In the rapidly evolving realm of cryptocurrencies, news and events serve as catalysts that shape market sentiment and drive price movements. The ability to discern the significance of news, to employ strategic analysis methodologies, and to embrace a comprehensive perspective is pivotal for navigating this information-rich landscape. By staying informed, verifying information, and understanding the interplay between news and broader market trends, traders and investors equip themselves to make prudent decisions in a landscape where news can have a profound and lasting impact on the trajectory of cryptocurrencies and blockchain technology.

CHAPTER VIII

Trading and Investing Tips for Success

Common pitfalls to avoid in the cryptocurrency market

The world of cryptocurrencies is a realm of immense potential and unprecedented innovation, attracting diverse participants eager to seize the opportunities it offers. Yet, within the promises of wealth and technological advancement also lie hidden pitfalls that can ensnare the unwary and lead to financial loss and disillusionment. This section delves into the common pitfalls that participants in the cryptocurrency market should be cautious of, examining the dangers of herd mentality, inadequate research, overtrading, neglecting security measures, and the allure of quick riches.

Herd mentality, a psychological phenomenon where individuals follow the crowd's actions without careful consideration, is a common pitfall in the cryptocurrency market. Fueled by social media, forums, and news coverage, participants may succumb to the fear of missing out (FOMO) or the fear of loss (FOMO). This can lead to buying or selling decisions driven by emotions rather than rational analysis. Following the crowd without independent research can result in poor investment choices, contributing to price bubbles and crashes.

Lack of proper research is another prevalent pitfall in the cryptocurrency market. With thousands of cryptocurrencies available, each with distinct use cases and technologies, investors must thoroughly understand the projects they invest in. Failing to grasp the fundamentals, team qualifications, technology, adoption potential, and competitive landscape can lead to investments in projects with little substance or long-term viability. Sound research empowers investors to make informed decisions based on a project's merits rather than speculative trends.

Overtrading, driven by the allure of short-term gains, is a peril that often befalls both novice and experienced traders. Due to the volatile character of the cryptocurrency market, investors may be tempted to participate in excessive buying and selling, which can lead to a buildup of transaction costs and an unwarranted exposure to risk. Overtrading can also lead to emotional burnout, eroding focus and discipline. A prudent approach involves setting clear trading strategies, adhering to risk management principles, and recognizing that successful trading requires patience and restraint.

In a digital landscape where assets are stored in digital wallets, neglecting security measures can have devastating consequences. Cryptocurrency exchanges and wallets are frequent targets of hackers, and individuals who fail to implement robust security measures risk losing their investments. Failing to use two-factor authentication, storing private keys insecurely, or falling for phishing scams are examples of security lapses that can lead to loss. Adhering to strong security practices, such as using hardware wallets and secure passwords, is vital to safeguarding investments.

The allure of quick riches is a trap that has ensnared many in the cryptocurrency market. The stories of overnight millionaires from early investments in Bitcoin or other cryptocurrencies can lead to unrealistic expectations. While substantial gains are possible, pursuing quick wealth can lead to impulsive decisions, excessive risk-taking, and investing in projects without proper due diligence. It is essential to approach the market with a long-term perspective, recognizing that success in the cryptocurrency market requires patience, education, and careful consideration.

Navigating the regulatory landscape is a significant challenge in the cryptocurrency market. Failure to understand and comply with regulatory requirements can lead to legal troubles and financial losses. Some projects may face legal actions or be labeled as securities by regulatory bodies. Participants who fail to report and pay taxes on cryptocurrency gains may face legal consequences. Staying informed about the regulatory environment in one's jurisdiction and seeking legal counsel when necessary is crucial to avoid regulatory pitfalls.

Investing solely in one cryptocurrency or project, known as lack of diversification, can amplify risks. While a project might seem promising, market dynamics can change rapidly. Relying solely on one investment exposes participants to the project's specific risks and vulnerabilities. Diversifying a portfolio across different projects and asset types can help mitigate risks associated with individual project failures or market volatility.

Emotional decision-making is a pitfall that can lead to impulsive actions and losses in the cryptocurrency market. Fear and greed, common emotions in trading, can cloud judgment and lead to irrational buying or selling decisions. Successful participants in the market cultivate emotional discipline, setting clear strategies, sticking to risk management principles, and avoiding decisions driven solely by emotions.

The ever-evolving nature of the cryptocurrency market demands continuous education. A lack of understanding about blockchain technology, the mechanics of different cryptocurrencies, and market trends can result in uninformed decisions. Participants who fail to invest time in learning about the technology and the market dynamics may make ill-informed choices, leading to financial losses.

The cryptocurrency market presents a realm of incredible opportunities and remarkable innovation. However, it is rife with pitfalls that can lead to financial loss, disillusionment, and even legal troubles. By avoiding the dangers of herd mentality, conducting thorough research, practicing restraint in trading, prioritizing security measures, steering clear of the allure of quick riches, understanding regulatory obligations, embracing diversification, cultivating emotional discipline, seeking continuous education, and approaching the market with a rational mindset, participants can navigate the complexities of the cryptocurrency landscape with greater resilience and the potential for more informed and successful decisions.

Strategies for buying and selling Bitcoin effectively

The cryptocurrency landscape, led by Bitcoin, is a realm of immense potential and substantial risk. For those venturing into this dynamic market, strategies for buying and selling Bitcoin effectively are not just advisable but essential. The intricate interplay of market volatility, technological innovation, and regulatory shifts demands a thoughtful approach considering both short-term gains and long-term growth. In this section, we delve into a spectrum of strategies designed to empower individuals to navigate the challenges of the cryptocurrency market, from the allure of day trading to the wisdom of HODLing, from the intricacies of technical analysis to the insights of fundamental analysis.

Day trading, characterized by frequent buying and selling within a single day, can be enticing due to the prospect of quick profits. This strategy leverages the market's volatility to capitalize on short-term price fluctuations. However, it requires a keen understanding of technical analysis, the ability to react swiftly, and an aptitude for managing stress. Day trading can be risky, with the potential for substantial losses, particularly for inexperienced traders who may fall victim to emotional decision-making or overtrading.

A more measured approach is required for swing trading, which seeks to profit from price fluctuations that take place over a period of a few days to a few weeks. Traders seek to identify trends and capitalize on price movements during these intermediate periods. While it requires a grasp of technical analysis and market trends, swing trading offers more flexibility than day trading. It's important to remember that even with a well-devised strategy, not all trades will yield gains, and proper risk management remains crucial.

The phrase "HODL," which is derived from an incorrect spelling of "hold," has developed into a slogan for long-term investors in the market for cryptocurrency. This approach involves buying and holding onto Bitcoin for an extended period, irrespective of short-term price fluctuations. HODLers focus on the long-term potential of Bitcoin, believing in its fundamental value proposition and the growing mainstream adoption. This strategy requires patience and a conviction in the transformative power of blockchain technology. While HODLing may involve enduring periods of market volatility, it can be a less stressful strategy than day or swing trading.

The term "dollar-cost averaging" refers to a strategy that reduces the negative effects of market volatility by investing the same amount of money at predetermined intervals, this is done regardless of the price of Bitcoin. This method ensures that investors accumulate Bitcoin over time, buying more when prices are low and less when prices are high. DCA minimizes the risk of making poor investment decisions based on short-term price fluctuations and helps manage emotional responses to market volatility. It is an approach that suits those who prioritize consistency and long-term growth over short-term gains.

Technical analysis involves studying historical price data and market trends to predict future price movements. Traders using this strategy use moving averages, trend lines, and chart patterns to identify potential entry and exit points. Although it is not foolproof, technical analysis can be a helpful instrument for gaining valuable insights into the state of the market and supporting better informed trading decisions. Traders must remain diligent in learning and adapting to changing market conditions to utilize technical analysis effectively.

Fundamental analysis is a strategy that assesses the intrinsic value of Bitcoin by evaluating its underlying technology, adoption potential, use cases, and overall market positioning. This approach requires a deep understanding of blockchain technology, the cryptocurrency ecosystem, and broader economic trends. Fundamental analysts monitor protocol upgrades, regulatory changes, partnerships, and adoption trends to gauge Bitcoin's long-term viability. While it may not offer immediate gains, fundamental analysis informs long-term investment decisions that align with a project's potential for growth.

Across all strategies, risk management is a cornerstone of successful Bitcoin trading and investment. Risk management involves setting clear parameters for capital allocation, determining acceptable levels of risk, and implementing strategies to limit potential losses. Stop-loss orders, diversification across assets, and avoiding the temptation of overleveraging are essential practices to protect one's investments and navigate the market's volatility responsibly.

Before implementing any strategy, it's paramount to educate oneself about Bitcoin, the blockchain, and the intricacies of the cryptocurrency market. A solid understanding of the technology and insights into market trends and regulatory developments are crucial for effective decision-making. Continuous learning and staying informed are vital components of an effective trading strategy.

Effectively buying and selling Bitcoin in the cryptocurrency market requires a deliberate approach that aligns with individual risk tolerance, investment objectives, and market knowledge. Whether one chooses day trading for quick gains, swing trading for more moderate profit opportunities, HODLing for long-term growth, or embraces the principles of dollar-cost averaging, technical analysis, or fundamental analysis, each strategy has its merits and considerations. Regardless of the chosen approach, risk management principles, ongoing education, and adaptability to evolving market conditions remain central to achieving success while minimizing risks. The cryptocurrency landscape is a dynamic realm, and while no strategy guarantees profits, thoughtful and disciplined approaches enhance the likelihood of making informed decisions in this ever-evolving and transformative domain.

Tips for staying updated and adapting to market changes

The world of cryptocurrency is a realm of unparalleled innovation and constant evolution. As the market ebbs and flows, staying updated and adapting to these rapid changes is not just beneficial but imperative for anyone seeking to navigate this dynamic landscape effectively. This section delves into a comprehensive array of tips that can empower individuals to stay informed about market trends, regulatory shifts, technological advancements, and emerging opportunities within the cryptocurrency realm. From leveraging news sources and social media to embracing educational platforms and community engagement, these strategies offer a roadmap for individuals to remain agile and proactive in an environment that rewards those who are well-informed.

Accessing information from diverse and reputable news sources is fundamental to staying updated in the cryptocurrency market. A mix of mainstream financial news outlets and specialized cryptocurrency publications ensures a balanced perspective. Platforms such as CoinDesk, Cointelegraph, and The Block provide insights into regulatory developments, market trends, and technological advancements. By cross-referencing information from multiple sources, individuals can sift through the noise and form a more accurate understanding of the current landscape.

Engaging with thought leaders and industry experts on social media platforms can provide useful insights into the cryptocurrency market. Twitter, in particular, serves as a hub for discussions, debates, and real-time updates from prominent figures in the industry. Following key personalities, developers, and researchers allows individuals to receive timely information, analyses, and expert opinions that contribute to a nuanced understanding of market dynamics.

Staying updated in the cryptocurrency space demands a commitment to continuous learning. Educational platforms such as online courses, webinars, and podcasts offer a structured way to expand one's knowledge. Platforms like Coursera, Udemy, and Khan Academy offer courses on blockchain technology, cryptocurrencies, and trading strategies. Engaging with these resources enhances understanding and equips individuals with the tools to make knowledgeable decisions.

Online forums and communities allow individuals to discuss trends, news, and insights in the cryptocurrency market. Platforms like Reddit, Bitcointalk, and Telegram host active communities where participants can share their perspectives, ask questions, and learn from others. Engaging in discussions fosters a sense of belonging and enables individuals to tap into collective wisdom, benefiting from diverse experiences and viewpoints.

Understanding technical and fundamental analysis is crucial for interpreting market trends and making informed decisions. Technical analysis involves studying price charts, identifying patterns, and using indicators to predict price movements. Fundamental analysis, on the other hand, involves assessing cryptocurrencies' underlying technology, adoption potential, and market positioning. Learning to conduct both types of analysis equips individuals with valuable tools for evaluating the market's trajectory.

Regulatory developments can significantly impact the cryptocurrency market. Staying informed about regulatory changes and legal frameworks is essential for making compliant and strategic decisions. Monitoring announcements from regulatory bodies, government statements, and legal experts helps individuals understand how evolving regulations may influence market dynamics and investment strategies.

Participating in cryptocurrency conferences and events provides an opportunity to connect with industry insiders, developers, and fellow enthusiasts. Events like Consensus, Blockchain Week, and DevCon offer a platform to learn about the most current trends, witness new product launches, and engage in networking opportunities. Conferences can provide invaluable insights, enabling individuals to grasp the pulse of the industry firsthand.

Market sentiment plays a pivotal role in cryptocurrency price movements. Platforms and tools that gauge market sentiment based on social media discussions, news coverage, and sentiment analysis algorithms offer insights into prevailing attitudes and emotions. Monitoring sentiment indicators helps individuals gauge the prevailing mood and adjust their strategies accordingly.

Crypto analytics platforms such as CoinMarketCap, CoinGecko, and TradingView provide real-time data, charts, and analytics for various cryptocurrencies. These platforms allow individuals to track price movements, trading volumes, market capitalization, and other relevant metrics. Utilizing such tools enables individuals to monitor market trends and make data-driven decisions.

Engaging with the cryptocurrency community through meetups, workshops, and online groups fosters connections and information sharing. Networking provides opportunities to learn from others, discuss trends, and gain insights from different perspectives. Individuals can stay updated on the latest developments and emerging opportunities by participating in the community.

In the fast-paced cryptocurrency market, adaptability is paramount. As trends evolve and new opportunities arise, being open to adjusting one's strategies and perspectives is crucial. Remaining flexible enables individuals to seize emerging trends and position themselves strategically.

Cryptocurrency investing and trading require a balance between short-term gains and long-term growth. While staying updated on short-term market trends is important, it's equally crucial to understand the long-term potential of cryptocurrencies and blockchain technology. Striking this balance enables individuals to make informed decisions aligning with their investment objectives.

Staying updated and adapting to market changes in the cryptocurrency realm is a multifaceted endeavor that requires a combination of strategies and approaches. From accessing diverse news sources, engaging with thought leaders, embracing educational platforms, and participating in online communities, individuals can understand market trends, technological shifts, and regulatory developments comprehensively. The cryptocurrency landscape is one of constant transformation, and those who invest in continuous learning, agile strategies, and a proactive mindset position themselves to navigate its intricacies effectively. By embracing these tips, individuals can stay ahead of the curve and navigate in this dynamic and transformative domain.

CHAPTER IX

Security and Best Practices for Bitcoin Owners

Importance of securing your Bitcoin holdings

In the ever-evolving landscape of cryptocurrency, Bitcoin stands as a beacon of financial autonomy and innovation. As individuals and institutions embrace the decentralized nature of digital assets, securing Bitcoin holdings has become a cornerstone of responsible engagement in this realm. This section delves into the multifaceted importance of safeguarding Bitcoin assets, exploring the complexities of cyber threats, vulnerabilities in digital infrastructure, the risks of centralized exchanges, and the vital role of private key management. From understanding the anatomy of a Bitcoin transaction to implementing robust security measures, this essay highlights the critical need for vigilance and education to navigate the digital frontier securely.

At the heart of Bitcoin's revolutionary framework lies its unique method of transaction verification—the blockchain. A decentralized and immutable ledger, the blockchain records every transaction ever conducted with Bitcoin. This provides an unparalleled level of transparency and accountability. However, this very feature underscores the need for securing Bitcoin holdings. Once a transaction is confirmed on the blockchain, it becomes irreversible, emphasizing the significance of adopting stringent security practices to prevent unauthorized access.

The digital era, with its unprecedented connectivity and accessibility, has ushered in a new generation of cyber threats. In order to gain illegal access to sensitive data, such as Bitcoin holdings, malicious actors take use of vulnerabilities in software, hardware, and the infrastructure of the network. Phishing attacks, malware, ransomware, and distributed denial-of-service (DDoS) attacks are just a few examples of tactics employed by cybercriminals. These threats underline the necessity of robust cybersecurity measures, emphasizing the importance of regular software updates, utilizing firewalls, and using secure browsing practices.

Centralized cryptocurrency exchanges are pivotal gateways for individuals to trade, buy, and sell Bitcoin. However, their centralized nature exposes users to substantial risks. Hacks on high-profile exchanges, which have resulted in the theft of Bitcoins worth millions of dollars, highlight the fragility of centralized platforms. Custodial exchanges control users' private keys and are particularly susceptible to breaches. As such, securing Bitcoin holdings involves minimizing exposure to exchanges and prioritizing using non-custodial wallets to store digital assets.

Central to the security of Bitcoin holdings is the concept of private keys. These cryptographic keys provide ownership and control over Bitcoin addresses, enabling transactions to be signed and verified. Securing private keys is paramount to preventing unauthorized access. These essential assets can be protected in a number of different ways, including by using hardware wallets, paper wallets, as well as cold storage systems. Hardware wallets, in particular, offer a secure offline environment for generating and storing private keys, effectively mitigating risks associated with online exposure. Multi-

signature wallets (multi-sig) offer an innovative approach to enhancing the security of Bitcoin holdings. In a multi-sig setup, multiple private keys are required to authorize a transaction, reducing the risk associated with a single point of failure. This mechanism is particularly valuable for institutional investors and businesses that need heightened security. Additionally, integrating Bitcoin into smart contracts expands security possibilities, allowing for programmable conditions to be met before transactions are executed.

Cold storage methods, involving the storage of private keys in an offline environment, offer a robust security solution. Hardware wallets, paper wallets, and air-gapped computers are common implementations of cold storage. Air-gapped computers, which are completely isolated from the internet, are especially effective in preventing remote attacks. Cold storage ensures that Bitcoin holdings remain impervious to online threats and vulnerabilities.

Bitcoin holdings are vulnerable to external threats and the potential for human error, accidents, and physical disasters. Implementing thorough backup and disaster recovery procedures is crucial. Creating redundant backups of private keys and recovery phrases, storing them in secure and geographically diverse locations, and regularly testing the recovery process helps mitigate the risks associated with data loss.

Adopting a proactive security mindset involves practicing good security hygiene. This includes employing strong and unique passwords, enabling two-factor authentication (2FA) wherever possible, and refraining from sharing sensitive information online. Furthermore, a commitment to continuous education and staying updated about emerging threats and best practices is instrumental in maintaining the security of Bitcoin holdings.

Central to the ethos of Bitcoin is the concept of financial sovereignty, where individuals become their own custodians. This decentralization extends to security practices. While centralized financial systems delegate security responsibilities to intermediaries, Bitcoin holders are responsible for securing their assets. This highlights the significance of education, empowerment, and the implementation of security methods that are in line with the ideas underlying decentralization.

As the world journeys into the era of digital finance, securing Bitcoin holdings emerges as an ethical responsibility and strategic imperative. The decentralized nature of Bitcoin, coupled with the vulnerability of digital infrastructure, necessitates a comprehensive approach to security. From understanding the intricacies of Bitcoin transactions to adopting multi-signature wallets, cold storage solutions, and practicing security hygiene, each step contributes to fortifying the protection of digital assets. The principles of ownership, empowerment, and vigilance are central to this endeavor. By embracing these principles and adopting robust security practices, individuals and institutions can confidently navigate cryptocurrency's evolving landscape, preserving the promise of financial autonomy in a digital age marked by both potential and peril.

Choosing a reliable wallet and implementing security measures

In the ever-evolving landscape of cryptocurrencies, the paramount importance of securing digital assets is a responsibility that cannot be understated. As individuals delve into the world of decentralized finance, the critical significance of selecting a trustworthy wallet and implementing robust security measures becomes a fundamental cornerstone of their journey. This section explores the intricate process involved in choosing a reliable wallet and navigating the intricacies of safeguarding cryptocurrency holdings. From comprehending the diverse types of wallets available to unraveling the layers of security best practices, this essay endeavors to equip individuals with the knowledge, tools, and strategies to protect their investments and confidently engage with the digital economy.

The array of wallet options stands as the initial threshold to securing cryptocurrency holdings. In the realm of cryptocurrencies, wallets are the digital apparatuses or hardware devices that facilitate storing, receiving, and transmitting digital assets. These wallets, ranging from software to hardware solutions, present distinct security and accessibility dimensions that necessitate careful consideration before adoption.

Software wallets, commonly called hot wallets, constitute a category encompassing applications and programs operational on internet-connected devices. Mobile wallets, desktop wallets, and online wallets, all falling under this classification, offer users convenience and accessibility, rendering them suitable for routine transactions. On the other hand, because they are always connected to the internet, these wallets are at risk of being attacked by malicious software.

In contrast, hardware wallets, also known as cold wallets, proffer a different perspective on securing cryptocurrency holdings. These tangible devices, resembling USB drives, introduce an offline storage solution that generates and retains private keys away from online exposures. This detachment from the internet renders hardware wallets particularly impervious to online threats, positioning them as ideal choices for extended storage durations and substantial sums of cryptocurrency.

A more traditional approach to wallet security involves paper wallets. Generating a cryptocurrency address and its associated private key on paper introduces an offline element to the process. This technique, although remarkably secure due to the absence of digital storage, requires meticulous handling to prevent damage or misplacement, as the physical medium is susceptible to wear and tear.

In a digital landscape where online convenience intersects with security complexities, web wallets emerge as a significant option. These wallets, hosted by third-party service providers on online platforms, deliver convenient ways of managing digital assets. However, their reliance on external platforms introduces an element of risk, potentially exposing users to hacking attempts and security vulnerabilities. While suitable for smaller cryptocurrency holdings intended for immediate transactions, their usage for more extensive or long-term holdings warrants careful consideration.

Furthermore, cryptocurrency exchanges often provide wallets as a supplementary service to users, enabling them to store their digital assets within the exchange environment. This convenience, however, presents a trade-off in terms of security. Exchanges control the private keys associated with these wallets, thereby placing the security of users' holdings in the hands of the exchange itself. Notoriously susceptible to hacking attempts, exchanges have witnessed high-profile breaches that have resulted in significant losses. Consequently, it is advised to utilize self-controlled wallets, where individuals retain full ownership and control over their private keys, for enhanced security.

The process of selecting a reliable wallet intertwines with the principles of security, and this intersection lays the groundwork for safeguarding cryptocurrency holdings from the perils of the digital realm. Embracing this intersection necessitates understanding private key security, a foundation upon which the security of cryptocurrency holdings is erected. Private keys are cryptographic elements that authenticate ownership and control over cryptocurrency addresses. Securing private keys is instrumental in preventing unauthorized access to digital assets.

By their very design, hardware wallets engender an environment that promotes the secure storage of private keys. These physical devices, often akin to USB drives, generate and house private keys offline, rendering them impervious to online threats. The absence of an online connection effectively mitigates the risks associated with cyberattacks, thus enhancing the security of private keys.

For those who opt for software wallets, the practice of implementing robust private key security becomes paramount. Storing private keys in encrypted formats, leveraging secure and unique passwords, and refraining from sharing private key information are crucial strategies in this regard. Employing hardware encryption mechanisms or utilizing secure operating systems further fortifies the protection of private keys within the software wallet ecosystem.

In tandem with private key security, implementing two-factor authentication (2FA) constitutes a formidable layer of defense. 2FA involves integrating an additional verification step before granting access to a wallet or online account. This supplementary layer of protection requires users to furnish a second form of verification—typically a unique code sent to their mobile device—alongside their primary password. The significance of 2FA lies in its ability to thwart unauthorized access, even when passwords may have been compromised due to external breaches.

The practice of secure backup and recovery serves as a contingency strategy against data loss—a scenario that could result in the irreversible forfeiture of cryptocurrency holdings. Creating secure backups of essential wallet information, encompassing private keys, recovery phrases, and authentication credentials, establishes a safety net to mitigate the consequences of unforeseen incidents. Geographically dispersing these backups and storing them in physically secure locations further augments the efficacy of this approach.

Regular updates to wallet software and firmware occupy a pivotal position in the realm of security measures. Developers continuously release updates that incorporate bug fixes, security enhancements, and patches to vulnerabilities that may have been identified. Consistently updating wallet applications ensures that potential vulnerabilities are promptly addressed and remediated, thus curtailing the risk of exploitation by cybercriminals seeking to exploit weaknesses in outdated versions.

The battle against cyber threats extends to the realm of social engineering, with phishing scams constituting a pervasive threat in the cryptocurrency space. Phishing attacks are conducted by malevolent entities who use deceptive methods to trick consumers into giving personal information or unintentionally sending cryptocurrency to fraudulent accounts. This underscores the necessity for individuals to exercise caution, engage in due diligence, and scrutinize the authenticity of communication channels before sharing personal data or responding to unsolicited requests.

Beyond the digital frontier, the security of cryptocurrency holdings is intertwined with the devices that serve as conduits for their management. Employing secure operating systems, leveraging up-to-date antivirus software, and configuring firewalls collectively contribute to establishing a fortified digital environment. Ensuring that devices remain free from malware and intrusions is an essential preemptive measure against threats that may seek to exploit vulnerabilities within the digital ecosystem.

Diversification, as a principle of risk mitigation, resonates within the realm of cryptocurrency security. Dividing holdings across multiple wallets, each employing distinct security mechanisms, contributes to a decentralized distribution of risk. Multi-signature wallets (multi-sig), a sophisticated concept within the realm of cryptocurrency security, exemplify this principle. In a multi-sig setup, multiple private keys are required to authorize a transaction, effectively diminishing the potential risk associated with a single point of failure.

However, the pursuit of wallet security transcends the realm of technology. It beckons individuals to embark on a journey of continuous education and vigilance. The landscape of cryptocurrencies is perpetually evolving, marked by the emergence of novel threats, developing hacking techniques, and innovative security solutions. Embracing a proactive approach to security mandates ongoing engagement with educational resources, online communities, and trusted sources of information. Staying informed equips individuals with the insights necessary to adapt their security strategies in response to the ever-changing threat landscape.

In conclusion, the significance of selecting a reliable wallet and implementing robust security measures reverberates as a foundational pillar within the cryptocurrency ecosystem. The diversity of wallet options, ranging from software and hardware wallets to paper and web wallets, empowers individuals to tailor their security approach according to their unique requirements and risk tolerance. Within this realm, private key security, two-factor authentication, secure backup procedures, and deploying secure operating systems all occupy integral positions in the arsenal of security best practices. Navigating the dynamic intersection of technology and vigilance, individuals possess the means to safeguard their cryptocurrency holdings from the multifaceted challenges posed by a digital landscape characterized by both boundless potential and lurking threats.

Protecting against scams and phishing attempts

The cryptocurrency landscape, marked by its transformative potential and decentralized nature, also harbors a dark underbelly characterized by scams and phishing attempts. As the digital frontier of finance continues to expand, so does the threat landscape that preys on unsuspecting individuals navigating the intricate pathways of the crypto space. This section embarks on a comprehensive exploration of the multifaceted world of scams and phishing within the realm of cryptocurrencies, unraveling the nuanced forms these threats take, the tactics employed by malicious actors, and the strategies that individuals can adopt to fortify their defenses and engage with confidence in the ever-evolving digital financial ecosystem.

In the dynamic arena of cryptocurrencies, the surge of innovation and opportunity has been met with an equivalent rise in fraudulent activities. Scams and phishing attempts have taken center stage as major concerns within the crypto space. From Ponzi schemes and fake initial coin offerings (ICOs) to elaborate phishing websites and social engineering tactics, the spectrum of scams reflects the diversity of opportunities in the cryptocurrency realm. These nefarious activities target both newcomers and seasoned participants, exploiting the complexities of digital finance and the allure of substantial profits.

At the heart of the scams and fraudulent activities lie various tactics employed by malicious actors. Impersonation, a prevalent approach, involves scammers masquerading as respected individuals or reputable organizations within the crypto community. By leveraging these fabricated personas, scammers create an illusion of trust, leading victims to fall prey to deceptive investments or divulge sensitive information. Fraudulent ICOs, an embodiment of this tactic, capitalize on the excitement and anticipation surrounding new cryptocurrency projects, luring victims with the promise of excessive returns. These schemes exploit the allure of quick riches in a landscape known for its potential to disrupt traditional finance.

Phishing, a term originating from the idea of "fishing" for victims, has found a sinister new form in the digital realm. This tactic involves the creation of imitation websites, emails, or messages that closely mimic legitimate sources. Victims are then directed to these fake platforms, where they're prompted to disclose private keys, passwords, or other confidential information. The growth of decentralized finance (DeFi) has expanded the horizons of phishing, with attackers exploiting vulnerabilities in smart contracts or enticing users into engaging with malicious decentralized applications (dApps). The speed of innovation in the crypto space, while opening doors to new possibilities, also opens windows for malicious actors to exploit vulnerabilities.

The realm of scams extends beyond technological subterfuge, delving into the psychological realm through social engineering. Social engineering relies on manipulation and trust-building, enticing individuals to part with their cryptocurrency holdings voluntarily. Scammers manipulate emotions, urgency, and the desire for quick profits to persuade victims to transfer funds to seemingly legitimate addresses. This form of manipulation often leaves victims blaming themselves for their losses, as they willingly participated in the transaction.

In the face of these multifaceted threats, proactive measures are pivotal in safeguarding against scams and phishing attempts. The foundation of a robust defense strategy rests on education and awareness. Individuals must familiarize themselves with common forms of scams and phishing tactics, enabling them to recognize red flags, question unusual requests, and critically evaluate investment opportunities. As the crypto space evolves, staying informed about emerging threats becomes an ongoing responsibility.

Vigilance serves as the first line of defense against scams and phishing. Verifying the authenticity of communication channels, websites, and social media accounts is a crucial practice. Established individuals and organizations within the crypto community often have verified accounts or official websites with SSL certificates, while fraudulent websites may display inconsistencies or employ unconventional domain names. Engaging in thorough due diligence before clicking on links or sharing personal information is a prudent step toward avoiding potential traps.

Multi-factor authentication (MFA) emerges as a powerful shield against unauthorized access. Enabling MFA on all accounts requires users to provide a second form of verification—usually a code sent to a mobile device—in addition to their password. Even fraudsters who are able to gain login credentials will have a difficult time breaking through this additional barrier brought about by this additional layer of security. It's a simple yet effective measure that significantly enhances account security.

The bedrock of cryptocurrency security lies in safeguarding private keys and recovery phrases. These elements grant control over one's cryptocurrency holdings and must be treated carefully. Hardware wallets, designed to securely store private keys offline, provide a physical barrier against online threats. Recovery phrases, often comprised of a sequence of words, should be stored in secure locations away from prying eyes and potential threats.

An unwavering principle in crypto is to avoid unsolicited offers and investment opportunities. Scammers often approach individuals with enticing proposals of high returns or exclusive investment opportunities. Verifying the legitimacy of these offers through trusted sources, seeking expert advice, and conducting due diligence helps individuals avoid falling victim to fraudulent schemes. It is essential to approach any potential investment opportunity with a healthy amount of skepticism and a commitment to verify information before making a decision to invest.

However, the responsibility of countering scams and phishing attempts doesn't solely rest on individuals. A collective effort to educate and inform others is a potent means of defense. Sharing knowledge about scams, phishing tactics, and common red flags with friends, family, and crypto community members builds a network of informed individuals who can collectively identify and report suspicious activities. A community armed with knowledge becomes a formidable barrier against the activities of malicious actors.

In conclusion, the evolving landscape of cryptocurrencies presents a complex challenge—fraudulent schemes and phishing attempts that exploit the boundless potential of digital finance. As individuals engage with the crypto space, education, vigilance, and proactive measures emerge as the cornerstones of defense against these threats. Recognizing the tactics of scams, verifying the authenticity of sources, implementing security measures like MFA and private key protection, and sharing knowledge within the community all contribute to a safer and more secure digital financial ecosystem. While the allure of innovation and financial freedom remains potent, the vigilance of individuals remains the ultimate shield against the shadowy realm of scams and phishing. As the crypto landscape matures, the fortitude of its participants in countering these threats will stand as a testament to the resilience of the digital financial revolution.

CHAPTER X

The Future of Bitcoin and Cryptocurrencies

Bitcoin's potential impact on the global financial system

The rise of Bitcoin has marked a seismic shift in the global financial landscape, sparking conversations and debates about its potential to revolutionize established norms and systems. This section delves deep into Bitcoin's potential impact on the global financial system, exploring its ripple effects on traditional finance, technological innovation, regulatory dynamics, and socio-economic transformations. As the pioneer of cryptocurrencies, Bitcoin has opened the doors to a decentralized future that challenges traditional paradigms and envisions a new era of financial possibilities.

At the heart of Bitcoin's influence lies its ability to disrupt traditional financial intermediaries. The centralized nature of legacy financial institutions, often characterized by banks, payment processors, and clearinghouses, has long been criticized for its inefficiencies, high fees, and exclusivity. Bitcoin's underlying technology, the blockchain, presents an alternative avenue for transactions and settlements that bypasses intermediaries. This revolutionary approach has the potential to streamline peer-to-peer transactions across borders, reduce friction, minimize costs, and expedite settlement times. As individuals and businesses experience the direct benefits of this disruption, traditional financial institutions may be compelled to adapt or reinvent their roles in this emerging landscape.

A core facet of Bitcoin's impact lies in its power to foster financial inclusion and empowerment on a global scale. Bitcoin provides a means for people to participate in the global economy even in parts of the world where traditional financial services are difficult to access. With just a smartphone and a Bitcoin wallet, individuals can engage in transactions, accumulate savings, and explore investment opportunities. The impact is particularly significant in remittance markets, notorious for high fees and extended wait times. Bitcoin's instantaneous and cost-effective cross-border transactions provide a lifeline to individuals seeking to transfer funds to loved ones worldwide. By democratizing financial access, Bitcoin has the potential to uplift marginalized populations, amplify economic opportunities, and contribute to socio-economic development.

Bitcoin's rise also holds implications for the concept of monetary sovereignty and the dynamics of global reserve currencies. Governments have begun exploring alternatives to assert greater control over their monetary policies in a world often dominated by the US dollar. With its decentralized nature and fixed supply, Bitcoin presents itself as a store of value that can transcend the uncertainties and inflation risks associated with traditional fiat currencies. This has led to discussions of "de-dollarization," where countries consider diversifying their reserves with digital assets, potentially reconfiguring the balance of power in the global economic landscape.

However, as Bitcoin's influence grows, it raises questions about financial stability and the necessity for regulatory frameworks. Regulatory authorities face the complex challenge of fostering innovation while safeguarding the financial system from market manipulation, money laundering, and investor protection risks. Striking the right balance between regulatory clarity and technological advancement is crucial in determining Bitcoin's integration into the broader financial ecosystem. Countries and jurisdictions are developing frameworks that mitigate risks and capitalize on the transformative potential of Bitcoin and blockchain technology.

Beyond its impact on traditional finance, Bitcoin's ascent has catalyzed a wave of technological innovation and infrastructure evolution. The underlying blockchain technology has far-reaching implications, extending beyond finance into supply chain management, voting systems, and secure digital identities. As industries tap into the potential of blockchain, they're poised for revolutionary changes in how they operate. Moreover, Bitcoin's rise has given birth to a burgeoning cryptocurrency ecosystem, fostering the creation of diverse financial products, services, and platforms that transcend traditional boundaries. This ecosystem nurtures innovation and collaboration, enabling individuals to access various financial tools and services.

However, the journey of integrating Bitcoin into the global financial system has challenges and limitations. Scalability remains a persistent concern, with the Bitcoin network's current architecture struggling to accommodate a high volume of transactions. The amount of energy that is consumed when mining Bitcoins has also come under examination, which has led to concerns regarding the cryptocurrency's impact on the environment and its long-term viability. Additionally, the volatility of Bitcoin's value presents challenges in its adoption as a stable store of value or medium of exchange. Regulatory hurdles, security vulnerabilities, and technology's dynamic evolution further add complexity to the integration process.

In conclusion, Bitcoin's meteoric rise has sparked a transformative dialogue about its potential impact on the global financial system. Its disruption of traditional intermediaries, empowerment of the underserved, and challenges to established monetary norms have far-reaching implications. However, this impact is nuanced, shaped by technological advancements, regulatory considerations, and the ever-evolving global financial landscape. Bitcoin's emergence beckons governments, financial institutions, technology pioneers, and society at large to collaborate in shaping a future where traditional and decentralized systems coexist harmoniously. As the dialogue continues to unfold, the potential of Bitcoin to reshape financial paradigms remains an exciting prospect, igniting innovation, fostering inclusivity, and pushing the boundaries of what's possible in the world of finance.

Regulatory challenges and prospects for the future

The ascent of Bitcoin has ushered in a new era of financial innovation and disruption, but it has also ignited a complex web of regulatory challenges that governments, financial institutions, and industry stakeholders must navigate. This section delves into the intricate landscape of Bitcoin's regulatory environment, examining the diverse approaches taken by different countries, the underlying concerns driving regulatory actions, and the potential avenues for shaping a regulatory framework that balances innovation, consumer protection, and financial stability.

As Bitcoin gains prominence on the global stage, a patchwork of regulatory approaches has emerged, reflecting the unique challenges posed by this decentralized digital currency. Countries worldwide have adopted varied stances towards Bitcoin, ranging from embracing its potential to introducing cautious regulatory measures. While some nations recognize Bitcoin as an innovative force that can transform financial systems, others raise concerns about its potential for money laundering, terrorist financing, and other illicit activities. The decentralized and borderless nature of Bitcoin complicates matters, as regulations in one jurisdiction may not suffice to address its cross-border impact.

Regulatory concerns surrounding Bitcoin are multifaceted and encompass a spectrum of issues. The pseudonymous nature of transactions raises worries about its susceptibility to misuse for criminal activities, including money laundering and tax evasion. The volatile nature of Bitcoin's value, which can experience significant fluctuations in short periods, presents challenges for market integrity and investor protection. Moreover, the uncharted territory of decentralized finance poses questions about investor education, disclosure, and risk management.

Countries have adopted a range of regulatory strategies in response to these concerns. Some nations have embraced a permissive approach, allowing innovation to flourish while implementing mechanisms to ensure consumer protection and market transparency. In contrast, others have enacted stringent regulations to curb the growth of Bitcoin and related services. These measures often arise from concerns about financial stability, capital flight, and the potential destabilization of traditional financial systems.

The challenge of regulating Bitcoin lies in balancing fostering innovation and safeguarding against risks. Regulatory authorities face the task of designing frameworks encouraging technological advancement while preventing illicit activities. One approach is establishing technology-neutral regulations focusing on outcomes rather than specific technologies. This approach allows for flexibility and adaptation as the cryptocurrency landscape evolves. Moreover, a harmonized international approach to regulation is crucial, as Bitcoin's borderless nature necessitates collaboration among countries to mitigate cross-border risks and regulatory arbitrage.

The future of Bitcoin regulation holds both challenges and opportunities. As the ecosystem evolves, regulatory approaches are likely to become more sophisticated and nuanced. Regulatory sandboxes, controlled environments that allow companies to test new products and services under regulatory guidance, could play a pivotal role in shaping effective regulations that encourage innovation while maintaining oversight. Furthermore, the emergence of central bank digital currencies (CBDCs) may influence the regulatory landscape, as governments seek to balance CBDCs and privately issued cryptocurrencies.

Education and industry engagement are vital components in shaping effective regulation. Regulators need a deep understanding of blockchain technology, cryptocurrencies, and their potential applications. Similarly, the cryptocurrency industry must actively engage with regulators to provide insights, share best practices, and contribute to developing regulations that strike the right balance. This collaboration can foster an environment of trust and cooperation, enabling regulators to make informed decisions that consider both innovation and risk mitigation.

Global regulatory coordination is essential to address the challenges posed by Bitcoin's borderless nature. When it comes to developing worldwide standards for anti-money laundering (or AML) and combating the financing of terrorism (or CFT) measures that extend to cryptocurrencies, international organizations such as the Financial Action Task Force (or FATF) play a vital role in the promotion of these measures. This coordinated effort helps establish consistent rules across jurisdictions and enhances information sharing to combat illicit activities.

In conclusion, Bitcoin's regulatory challenges reflect the complexities of regulating a decentralized and innovative technology within a globalized financial landscape. Striking a balance between encouraging innovation and mitigating risks requires dynamic and adaptive approaches. Collaboration among regulators, industry stakeholders, and technology experts is crucial to shaping a regulatory framework that promotes innovation while safeguarding against financial crime and market instability. As governments and regulators grapple with the complexities of Bitcoin's emergence, their decisions will shape the future of cryptocurrencies and the broader financial ecosystem for years to come.

Other promising cryptocurrencies and projects to watch

In the vast landscape of cryptocurrencies, many projects beyond Bitcoin have emerged, each with the potential to reshape industries, revolutionize financial systems, and drive technological innovation. This section delves into the world of promising cryptocurrencies and projects that have captured the attention of investors, innovators, and enthusiasts. From Ethereum's pioneering smart contracts to the disruptive potential of decentralized finance (DeFi) platforms and beyond, these projects embody the evolution of blockchain technology and its transformative impact on various sectors.

Ethereum, often hailed as Bitcoin's successor, is a beacon of innovation with its groundbreaking concept of smart contracts. Going beyond the scope of Bitcoin's capabilities, Ethereum let developers to create decentralized applications (DApps) that can execute complex operations automatically and autonomously. This innovative leap has laid the foundation for the explosive growth of DeFi, allowing users to access myriad financial services without traditional intermediaries. With its ongoing transition to Ethereum 2.0, the platform aims to address scalability, energy efficiency, and security concerns, cementing its role as a leading platform for blockchain innovation.

DeFi, a seismic shift in the financial landscape, has garnered significant attention by harnessing blockchain technology to create an open and permissionless financial services ecosystem. Projects such as MakerDAO, Aave, and Compound have introduced novel concepts like algorithmic stablecoins and lending protocols, enabling users to earn interest, borrow assets, and participate in decentralized governance. This surge in DeFi platforms has the potential to democratize financial services globally, providing individuals worldwide with access to opportunities previously confined to traditional financial institutions.

Polkadot emerges as a distinct player in the cryptocurrency realm by addressing a fundamental challenge: interoperability between different blockchains. The project's innovative architecture enables diverse blockchains to seamlessly connect and share information, fostering a multi-chain ecosystem where specialized blockchains can collaborate and interact synergistically. Polkadot's emphasis on interoperability opens the doors to increased efficiency, scalability, and innovation, as projects can leverage the strengths of various blockchains within a unified framework.

Cardano sets itself apart by adopting a scientific approach to blockchain development. Its commitment to peer-reviewed research and formal verification methods aims to create a more secure and scalable blockchain. Cardano's multi-layered architecture prioritizes scalability, sustainability, security, and regulatory compliance, offering a comprehensive solution to the challenges faced by earlier blockchains. With its emphasis on research-backed innovation, Cardano positions itself as a project to watch for advancements in blockchain technology.

Solana has carved a niche for itself in the cryptocurrency arena by focusing on scalability and high throughput. Its unique consensus mechanism, Proof of History, is designed to enhance transaction speeds and reduce latency, addressing the scalability concerns many blockchain platforms face. Solana's architecture lends itself to developing resource-intensive decentralized applications and protocols, attracting developers seeking fast and efficient execution for their projects.

Filecoin tackles the challenge of decentralized data storage by creating a marketplace where individuals and organizations can buy and sell storage space. The goal of the project is to create a decentralized and highly secure network for storing and retrieving data, and it does this by utilizing blockchain technology. With its innovative approach to cloud storage, Filecoin has the potential to revolutionize data storage services, shifting control from centralized entities to a decentralized network of storage providers.

The function that Chainlink plays as a connection between smart contracts and real-world data is at the heart of its distinctive value proposition. Smart contracts on blockchain platforms often lack access to external information, limiting their potential applications. Chainlink addresses this limitation by providing a decentralized oracle network that connects smart contracts with real-world data sources, enabling them to interact with external data and execute more sophisticated tasks autonomously and securely.

In the realm of blockchain ecosystems, Binance Smart Chain (BSC) has emerged as a competitor to Ethereum, offering an alternative for developers and users seeking faster transaction speeds and lower fees. BSC combines the benefits of smart contract functionality with reduced congestion, making it an attractive platform for decentralized applications and DeFi projects. Its growing ecosystem of applications and protocols positions BSC as a contender in the DeFi space and a potential driver of innovation within the broader cryptocurrency landscape.

In conclusion, the world of cryptocurrencies has evolved far beyond Bitcoin's pioneering days, ushering in a diverse array of promising projects that leverage blockchain technology to reimagine industries, redefine financial systems, and drive technological progress. Ethereum's smart contracts, the DeFi revolution, projects like Polkadot, Cardano, Solana, Filecoin, Chainlink, and Binance Smart Chain represent a mere fraction of the dynamic projects capturing the imagination of investors and enthusiasts alike. As these projects continue to mature, gain traction, and push the boundaries of innovation, they underscore blockchain technology's versatility and transformative potential. The ongoing evolution of the cryptocurrency ecosystem is poised to reshape traditional paradigms, foster unprecedented innovation, and provide a glimpse into a future where decentralized technologies shape the fabric of various aspects of our lives.

CONCLUSION

Recap of key strategies and insights for success in the cryptocurrency market

A comprehensive understanding of the cryptocurrency market's complexities, risks, and possibilities is required in order to successfully navigate the market's ever- shifting terrain, which is notoriously difficult to comprehend. This section provides a recap of essential strategies and insights that are crucial for achieving success in this dynamic market. From foundational principles such as risk management and due diligence to advanced techniques like technical analysis and market sentiment assessment, these strategies serve as a compass for individuals seeking to thrive in cryptocurrencies' volatile yet promising realm.

The cornerstone of triumph in the cryptocurrency market is rooted in the principles of effective risk management and meticulous due diligence. The market's inherent volatility necessitates a prudent approach to capital allocation, highlighting the significance of diversification and setting clear investment goals. The ability to manage risks is underscored by an awareness of potential losses, urging investors only to commit funds they can afford to lose. Simultaneously, thorough due diligence, encompassing comprehensive research into projects, teams, and underlying technologies, is pivotal in identifying ventures with genuine value propositions and long-term viability.

Among the fundamental choices facing investors is the decision between a long-term "HODL" strategy and active engagement in short-term trading. Balancing these perspectives is integral to harnessing the strengths of both approaches. Long-term investors are positioned to capitalize on market cycles and potential substantial gains over time. In contrast, short-term traders leverage market fluctuations to realize swift profits, relying on a blend of technical and fundamental analysis to strategically time their trades. The equilibrium between these strategies hinges on aligning them with individual risk tolerance and investment objectives.

Technical analysis, a cornerstone of trading in financial markets, empowers cryptocurrency traders with the tools to interpret historical price data, identify patterns, and forecast potential future price movements. Vital technical indicators provide insights into market momentum and sentiment, including moving averages, the Relative Strength Index (RSI), and Bollinger Bands. A comprehensive grasp of chart patterns and a deep dive into technical analysis allow traders to make informed decisions regarding optimal entry and exit points. Nevertheless, the efficacy of technical analysis relies on a fusion of market sentiment, external events, and statistical probabilities.

A profound comprehension of market sentiment is a keystone in cryptocurrency, where emotions often sway decision-making. Analyzing market sentiment involves assessing the collective psychology of investors through various avenues, including social media analysis, sentiment indexes, and news sentiment. Positive sentiment often aligns with bullish trends, while a prevalence of negative sentiment may indicate impending corrections. Merging market sentiment analysis with technical and fundamental analysis yields a holistic understanding of the market landscape, aiding traders in making well-informed decisions.

Fundamental analysis, a bedrock of traditional financial markets, extends its influence to the cryptocurrency realm by evaluating the intrinsic value of cryptocurrencies and projects. Scrutinizing factors such as the team's expertise, project goals, technological innovations, partnerships, and community engagement is pivotal in distinguishing projects with authentic potential from those without substance. Fundamental analysis, integral to long-term investment strategies, is equally influential in short-term trading decisions as market participants respond to real-time project updates and significant news events.

Staying informed and adeptly adapting to market changes are cardinal strategies in the cryptocurrency market, where volatility and rapid shifts are constants. Sourcing information from reputable news outlets, social media, and community platforms is imperative in making well-informed decisions. Adapting to market changes requires vigilance in recognizing trends, regulation shifts, and technological advancements that can catalyze significant price movements. A blend of vigilance and agility, coupled with the capability to recalibrate strategies in response to new information, underscores the resilience of successful cryptocurrency traders.

Emotions and impulses often pose as pitfalls in the cryptocurrency market, potentially leading to irrational decisions and subsequent losses. The "Fear of Missing Out" (FOMO) frequently drives investors to enter positions at the height of bullish trends, only to witness losses as trends reverse. Navigating these challenges necessitates an unyielding commitment to disciplined and rational trading, adhering to pre-defined strategies, and sidestepping emotional decision-making.

The safety of investments is a paramount concern in the cryptocurrency market, given the prevalence of cyber threats and hacks. Opting for secure wallets, implementing robust security measures, and safeguarding private keys are critical steps in shielding investments from potential breaches. Utilizing cold wallets and hardware wallets offers added layers of security, keeping assets offline and beyond the reach of online vulnerabilities.

Long-term success in the cryptocurrency market hinges on the values of patience and continuous education. Market cycles, characterized by periods of exuberance and downturns, are an inherent part of the cryptocurrency ecosystem. The capability to endure market fluctuations with a long-term outlook is a defining trait of successful investors. Concurrently, a steadfast commitment to staying abreast of technological advancements, regulatory shifts, and industry trends equips investors with the adaptability required to thrive.

In conclusion, succeeding in the cryptocurrency market demands a multi-faceted strategy, encompassing risk management, technical analysis, market sentiment assessment, fundamental analysis, and the agility to stay informed and adapt. By adhering to foundational principles, sustaining a balanced perspective, and implementing strategies that align with personal objectives, investors can effectively navigate the volatility and uncertainty intrinsic to the market. As the cryptocurrency landscape undergoes constant transformation, the ability to learn, adapt, and execute effective strategies will remain instrumental in achieving success and harnessing this digital frontier's vast potential.

Encouragement for readers to take action and apply what they've learned

Embarking on the journey into the world of cryptocurrency entails more than just amassing knowledge; it's about translating that knowledge into action and embarking on a path of potential transformation. This section encourages readers to harness the insights gained from their exploration of cryptocurrencies and take proactive steps toward realizing their investment goals. By delving into actionable strategies, fostering a proactive mindset, and emphasizing the transformative power of execution, we seek to empower readers to navigate the complexities of the cryptocurrency market with confidence and conviction.

Pursuing knowledge is undoubtedly vital, but the true essence lies in the practical application of that knowledge. As readers delve into the intricacies of cryptocurrencies, blockchain technology, and investment strategies, the transition from learning to doing becomes the linchpin of success. This transformative journey is catalyzed when theoretical concepts are transformed into tangible actions that can potentially shape financial futures.

Taking that initial step may seem daunting, but the secret lies in starting small. In the cryptocurrency realm, where volatility and uncertainty are constants, a gradual approach aids in building confidence. Begin by dipping your toes into the market with a modest investment, allocating funds you are comfortable with. This mitigates risk and serves as a testing ground for your strategies and decision-making prowess.

Risk is an inherent component of any investment endeavor, yet the prospect of risk often deters individuals from taking action. However, embracing calculated risks is integral to growth. Readers can navigate the terrain with prudence by carefully assessing potential rewards against potential losses and leveraging the risk management strategies learned. After all, the most significant opportunities arise in the face of challenges and calculated risks.

As you embark on this transformative journey, having clear objectives acts as a compass. Define your investment goals, whether they involve short-term gains, long-term wealth accumulation, or participation in innovative projects. By setting specific, measurable, achievable, relevant, and time-bound (SMART) goals, you imbue your actions with purpose and direction, aligning your efforts with your overarching vision.

Diversification is the bedrock of a resilient investment portfolio. Having acquired insights into cryptocurrencies' diversity and potential applications, readers can strategically allocate funds across various assets. This safeguards against the impact of a single asset's poor performance while capitalizing on the growth of promising ventures. A well-diversified portfolio acts as a buffer against volatility and offers a balanced exposure to different market segments.

The cryptocurrency market is constantly in flux, demanding a dynamic mindset from its participants. Readers are encouraged to remain adaptable, consistently learning, and evolving their strategies in response to new information, emerging trends, and changing market conditions. Such an approach enhances decision-making and aligns with the innovation ethos that defines the cryptocurrency landscape.

Education without action remains latent potential. While acquiring knowledge about cryptocurrency concepts, market dynamics, and investment strategies is essential, applying that knowledge is the true catalyst for change. Start by executing small trades, setting up secure wallets, and exploring projects aligned with your investment goals. By actualizing what you've learned, you transform theory into tangible results.

Inertia can be a formidable obstacle to progress. Readers are urged to overcome the inertia of indecision by taking that first step toward action. The momentum gained from one small success fuels further engagement, building confidence and setting the stage for more substantial accomplishments. Keep in mind that the first step of any journey is the most important, and that every action, no matter how insignificant it may seem, moves you one step closer to achieving your goals.

The cryptocurrency journey is akin to a marathon, not a sprint. Instant gratification may be elusive, but the cultivation of patience is its own reward. Encountering market fluctuations and unforeseen challenges is an integral part of the journey. Embrace setbacks as learning opportunities and stay committed to your long-term objectives. Patience acts as a guiding light in the face of volatility and uncertainty.

In the intricate tapestry of the cryptocurrency world, knowledge finds its true potency when it's woven into the fabric of action. This essay aims to encourage readers to traverse the threshold from learning to execution, offering actionable insights for entering the cryptocurrency market with confidence. By venturing into the world of cryptocurrencies armed with a proactive mindset, an understanding of risk and reward, and a commitment to continual learning and adaptation, readers possess the tools to navigate the complexities of the market and potentially transform their financial trajectories. Keep in mind that the proverbial "journey of a thousand miles begins with a single step," and in the world of cryptocurrencies, that step translates into the power of taking action that is both informed and purposeful.

Final thoughts on the significance of Bitcoin in the financial world

As we delve into the concluding reflections on the profound significance of Bitcoin in the financial world, a multifaceted tapestry of transformative impacts emerges. This section seeks to encapsulate the final thoughts on how Bitcoin has reshaped financial paradigms, challenged traditional systems, and ushered in a new era of possibilities. From its disruptive potential to the democratization of finance, from its role in technological innovation to its navigational challenges and future prospects, the significance of Bitcoin reverberates through the financial landscape as a symbol of change and a catalyst for reshaping the norms.

At the heart of Bitcoin's significance lies its role as a trailblazer in decentralization. Traditional financial systems have long relied on centralized control, where governments and financial institutions dictate monetary policies. Bitcoin's emergence shattered this model, introducing a decentralized architecture powered by blockchain technology. This shift has decentralized the power over transactions and monetary policies, fostering a more democratic and inclusive financial ecosystem. By sidestepping intermediaries and giving individuals greater control over their financial transactions, Bitcoin has ignited conversations about self-sovereignty and individual empowerment.

Bitcoin's impact extends beyond its technological underpinnings; it has emerged as a financial empowerment tool. Due to various barriers, the world's unbanked and underbanked populations have traditionally been excluded from formal financial systems. However, Bitcoin's borderless nature and accessibility have transcended geographical boundaries, opening avenues for financial inclusion. By adopting simple technologies like smartphones, individuals previously excluded from the financial discourse can now actively participate in the global economy. This newfound financial agency not only empowers individuals but also has the potential to reshape entire communities and economies.

As a disruptive force, Bitcoin has questioned long standing financial paradigms and conventions. Central banks have historically maintained the ability to manipulate monetary supply, often leading to economic fluctuations. Bitcoin's limited supply, capped at 21 million coins, challenges this practice by adhering to a deflationary model. This clash of inflationary and deflationary economic models has spurred debates about the broader implications for economic stability and growth. This disruption forces traditional financial institutions to reevaluate their practices and adopt more innovative and adaptive approaches to monetary policy.

The democratization of finance stands as a defining hallmark of Bitcoin's significance. Through fractional ownership and the rise of tokenization, Bitcoin has made it possible for individuals to participate in wealth-building endeavors that were previously out of reach. The fractional ownership of Bitcoin allows individuals to invest in small increments, thereby reducing barriers to entry for high-value assets. Moreover, the rise of Initial Coin Offerings (ICOs) and the creation of various tokens have expanded the concept of ownership beyond traditional assets. This democratization of ownership fosters a more equitable distribution of wealth and resources, challenging existing economic disparities.

Beyond its immediate impacts, Bitcoin has catalyzed an era of technological innovation. The invention of Bitcoin introduced the world to blockchain technology, a distributed and transparent ledger system that has since found applications far beyond the realm of finance. The immutable nature of blockchain technology has led to its acceptance in a variety of industries, spanning from supply chain management to healthcare, where it offers the promise of enhanced transparency, security, and efficiency. The rise of alternative cryptocurrencies and the development of decentralized applications (dApps) have further broadened the technological landscape, inspiring a new wave of digital transformation and innovation.

Navigating the regulatory challenges that accompany Bitcoin's rise has been an intricate journey.

Cryptocurrencies' decentralized and borderless nature has presented governments and regulatory bodies with unique challenges. Categorizing cryptocurrencies, establishing taxation frameworks, and ensuring consumer protection have been focal points of concern. Striking the balance between fostering innovation and safeguarding consumers requires cooperation and collaboration between various stakeholders, including governments, financial institutions, and the cryptocurrency community. The outcome of these regulatory dialogues will likely shape the trajectory of Bitcoin's integration into the global financial ecosystem.

As Bitcoin's journey unfolds, its significance is not limited to the present moment but extends to its possibilities for the future. However, challenges persist on this path of evolution. Scalability issues, energy consumption concerns, and the environmental impact of cryptocurrency mining are just a few of the hurdles that need to be overcome. The ongoing dialogue within the cryptocurrency community and the pursuit of innovative solutions underscores the commitment to continuous improvement and growth.

In conclusion, the significance of Bitcoin in the financial world is a narrative rich with themes of decentralization, inclusivity, disruption, and innovation. Its influence has gone beyond being just another form of currency; it has sparked conversations about redefining control, democratizing access, and reimagining financial systems. Bitcoin's journey has been one of transformation, presenting new possibilities and raising pertinent questions about the future of finance. As we reflect on the final thoughts regarding Bitcoin's significance, we are reminded of the profound impact it has already had and the immense potential it continues to hold. In embracing its transformative power, we pave the way for a financial future that is more equitable, inclusive, and adaptable to the changing tides of innovation.

Thank you for buying and reading/ listening to our book. If you found this book useful/ helpful please take a few minutes and leave a review on the platform where you purchased our book. Your feedback matters greatly to us.